Grandmothers

The Changing Culture

Geoff Dench
editor

Transaction Publishers
New Brunswick (U.S.A.) and London (U.K.)

Library of Congress Catalog Number: 2001041587
ISBN: 0-7658-0893-5
Printed in the United States of America

Library of Congress Cataloging-in-Publication Data

Grandmothers : the changing culture / Geoff Dench, editor.
    p. cm.
Includes bibliographical references and index.
ISBN: 0-7658-0893-5 (pbk. : alk. paper)
    1. Grandmothers—Great Britain. I. Dench, Geoff.

HQ759.9 .G7155 2001
306.874'5—dc21   2001041587

Grandmothers

Contents

EXPERIENCED HANDS

NEWER RECRUITS

ACKNOWLEDGEMENT

The Hera Trust is grateful to the Robert Gavron Charitable Trust for valued support in producing this collection.

PREFACE: WHY GRANDMOTHERS?

Geoff Dench

This book brings together a collection of personal reflections on what it means to be a grandmother in contemporary society, and views on how the role may be evolving.

We can safely assume from the outset that it will have changed a good deal in living memory, because family life in general has gone through radical transformations. Two sets of factors have been particularly important here. Firstly, developments in medical technology have helped to increase control over reproduction, so having a family can more easily be timed and scaled to fit in with other activities. Secondly, the growth of citizenship, as manifest in the multiplication of state supports, has meant that being a parent no longer need entail such dependence as before on relatives, friends and neighbours. Basic social security has become separated from community ties and obligations. Over the last third of a century these two major influences have combined to give people a larger choice of lifestyles, and thereby to encourage experimentation with new forms of household and family relationship.

Most commentaries on the ensuing lifestyle revolution have not touched on grandparents. But over the last few years there

Geoff Dench is a senior research fellow at the Institute of Community Studies, *and a professor of Sociology at* Middlesex University. *He has written several books on family relations and, before that, on race and ethnic relations.*

has been a surge of interest in grandparenting - prompted mainly by concern over the possible effects on children of new styles of parenting - and in the part that grandparents might play or be playing as saviours of family life.

In response to these concerns, the *Institute of Community Studies* and *National Centre for Social Research* carried out a survey to get some idea of the current role played by grandparents in British society. This has given us a solid general picture of how the role is now acted out, plus some fascinating hints about how it may be changing.[1] However one survey, conducted over one short period, cannot really tell us much about trends. To get more insight into questions of how the role is adapting to new family behaviour it seemed essential to ask people who have been grandparents through the lifestyle revolution to make some personal assessments.

The accounts which follow here will help to give our research the historical dimension it lacks. This will go beyond clarifying the part played by grandparents. It also involves providing commentaries on the wider transformation of family and sexual behaviour. No realistic assessment of a radical change in lifestyles can be started until it has been tested in all stages of life. Young people are usually more willing to adopt novel ideas, especially those which challenge authority structures and give short-cuts to independence. But until new ideas have been adapted to the needs of other age-groups too, and can be seen to allow co-operation between generations, they cannot be regarded as viable. Only as the cohort leading the revolution itself moves through the life-cycle does it become possible to see which of its practices are ephemeral and age-specific, and which are more general and sustainable.[2]

We are arriving at this defining stage now for the libertarian revolution which was launched in the sixties. The wartime and postwar babyboom cohorts have started to become grandparents and take on senior family positions. So we can now begin to see how far they will continue innovating and casting aside tradition, and how far the logic of their new roles may lead them back towards rediscovery and reassertion of traditional ways. It is an important moment of truth.

But why grand*mothers*?

THE ROUSING OF *MOTHER NATURE*

This opportunity for appraisal of social revolution coincides very handily with the rise of exciting new intellectual models, offering additional dimensions of analysis. The new discipline of Evolutionary Psychology, springing from the work of the late William Hamilton, has seriously challenged the traditional dichotomy between 'culture' (society) and 'nature'. This inevitably changes the way that we look at the sixties revolution. That was based on assertion of the power of human thought to transcend material factors, and to freely invent new futures. But as the wheel of revolution turns it is these new materialist theories which seem to offer the neater explanations of how society works. In particular, they are producing very stimulating insights into the part that women, and female nature, may have played in the formation of society.

One of the key debates here revolves, aptly enough, around the 'grandmother hypothesis'.[3] This debate springs out of scholarly efforts to understand the menopause. Human beings are one of the very few species where female fertility does not continue up to the end, or near the end, of the normal life-span. Elephants and whales share this. Excellent company!

The existence of the menopause is almost certainly linked with the importance of long-term mothering in species where the young are dependent for a long period. Mothers who have children late in life cannot hope to rear them all, and may die even younger themselves in the attempt. However, menopause may also, perhaps even more revealingly, be related to *grand*mothering - and an *overlapping* of mothering in two generations. A mother with young children whose own mother is still alive, and *not* tied down by young children of her own, can expect crucial help during the early years when her infant offspring are most demanding.

As a result, those women genetically programmed to lose their fertility relatively early in their lives may prove more likely to have descendants who thrive and survive to have offspring of their own - who then pass on those genes. Thus the evolution of the menopause may be part of the evolution of human family behaviour.

There is more. Most evolutionary psychologists are reluctant to speculate too far on this, but it does seem extremely likely that the key role occupied by grandmothers within family groups will have given them immense influence on the development and operation of community life more generally. We know from historians and anthropologists that grandmothers are extremely important as repositories and transmittors of culture. As noted by Marc Bloch:

> *'Before the institution of the newspaper, the primary school, and military service, the education of the youngest living generation was generally undertaken by the oldest living generation. In rural village societies, because working conditions kept mothers and fathers away almost all day, especially during the summer period, the young children were brought up chiefly by their grandparents; so that it is from the oldest member of the household that the memory of the group was mediated to them.... Until the introduction of the first machines, it was grandmother who was the mistress of the household, who prepared the meals, and who, alone, was occupied with the children. It was her task to teach the language of the group.'* [4]

GRANDMA KNOWS BEST

If transmittor, then why not formulator too? No other category of family member could have been even half as well-placed, or disposed, to reflect on and assess the fundamental social values and rules which make community life possible.

Consider the following. Grandmothers are generally the oldest members of a family group, with the greatest accumulation of personal experience. As women, their reproductive strategy entails long-term concern for the well-being of those around them. So they will also store knowledge about, and *care* about, the lives of many others in all age and sex categories.

On top of this, because they are (usually) no longer fertile themselves (and often widowed anyway) they are, more than old men, ideally suited to stand above or outside of the reproductive marketplace and to take an inclusive and integrating view of personal relationships. Looked at in this light, they are far better qualified and motivated than anyone else to devise reasonably objective schemes for the orderly management of family and sexual relations, which other family members could find acceptable.

Thus it is grannies who are typically the guardians of the common good and moral codes embodying this. They are the family peace-makers, match-makers and advisers. And while the primary reference of the principles they uphold will be inside families it is generally fairly obvious in most societies that *wider* moral systems, shaping relations between families and between other groups in the community, and informing law and religion, are themselves rooted in the rules of family life and its moral economy. All in all, the grandmother hypothesis provides ample encouragement for the general idea (which I have myself explored in an earlier book[5]) that it is women, and especially *older* women, who are the main authors of human culture and architects of social structure.

Do not be misled by the fact that cultures generally represent men as central. Much of this public 'theatre of patriarchy' may be myth, covering and compensating for men's actual marginality and helping to steer them into useful activity and commitment.

Some such refurbished notion of mother nature, or perhaps *grand*mother nature, as a fundamental aspect of society (rather than as something opposed to it) seems to be in the ascendant at the moment. It certainly appears capable of attracting wide acceptance. Not only does it build on the solid achievements of down-to-earth feminism over the last few decades in identifying contributions made by women to social development. It also helps to exorcise another, thoroughly *obscurantist* tradition of feminism influential over the same period, namely the *Flat-Earth* tendency which resolutely denies human sexual differences and attributes all variations in behaviour to 'social construction'.

This latter tradition, itself a legacy of sixties idealism, has arguably done much to delay the emergence of popular new conventions for family organisation, compatible with modern realities. The revolutionary battle cry that 'family' is just an instrument of male bourgeois cultural oppression still echoes in the corridors of Whitehall and Westminster, where it continues to trigger panic among policy-makers. If anything can silence this ghost, and usher in much-needed rehabilitation of consensual family policy, it is Grandmother Nature.

THE COLLECTION

This volume taps into a selection of grandmothers' experience of contemporary family life, and gives an indication of their concerns. (Some names have been changed to conceal identities and protect confidentiality.) A few of the authors are, inevitably, people with an existing involvement in the subject, and with a special interest in it. But we have tried to bring together contributors with a variety of perspectives and from a wide range of backgrounds. This does not, of course, make them a fully representative cross-section, containing the same balance of experiences and views as the general population. Nevertheless the collection should help to give a broad idea of how the role is changing.

To assist interpretation, the chapters are ordered according to the length of time spent as a grandmother. The first group, of *Veteran grandmothers*, have all done at least fifteen years active service. During that period they have assisted or witnessed many changes in family life, and coped with many of the consequences. *Experienced hands* have been grannies for around ten years or so, and *Newer recruits* for up to five.[6] None in the final batch, *Grandmothers-in-waiting*, are yet active grandmothers, but they will be soon or have started thinking about it.

This structure is mainly designed to help reveal how views on being a grandmother are influenced by experience of it. But inevitably, and perhaps running partly counter to this aim, it is also bound to pick up historical (or 'cohort') shifts in the expectations which grandmothers themselves bring to the role.

This is not the place for me to analyse contributors' views along either of these axes. Both as a man and non-grandparent I have to be careful not to influence too closely how particular chapters are read. They must speak for themselves. But I cannot refrain from making the general observation that much of what is expressed in many of them - in particular belief in the paramount *importance* of families in society, not just for the sake of their members but also for the common good - seems to run counter to received opinion about 'what women want' in modern society. The contents of this book clearly suggest to me an effective exclusion of older women's voices and views from influential contemporary social policy debates.

RECOVERING A VOICE

Older women belong at the heart of cultural and social debate. But in the west we have allowed their voices to become muffled and ignored and this represents, notwithstanding the lavish and visible attention given to the interests of younger women, a net diminution in women's position. In more traditional societies the public participation of women may often be minimal. But most women in them are accorded high status and respect, especially on moral questions. Many also exercise considerable influence through sons and husbands, and as family managers, on the conduct of wider public affairs.[7] The fading of this influence in the west, together with dismantling of the wider family systems through which it operates, constitute a lingering legacy of the sixties.

Such exclusion may have a point in the early stages of social revolution, when generations are divided on many issues and opposition to change by elders may be based solely on dogma. But that no longer applies in this case. The great majority of older women in the west, certainly the grandmothers, now have close personal experience of 'new family' life. Their views are grounded, and in no way out of touch. It is the current wave of grandmothers who, against a background of declining public respect for the 'private realm' of family life, have done much to hold families together during the last twenty to thirty years. They are not easily shocked; and if anyone knows what is possible in modern situations, and what the basic rules for sustainable family life need to be, then *they* are the experts. They are in the vanguard in making this revolution work.

Research in countries which are ahead of us in exploring these issues suggests that the cultural gap which undoubtedly existed between generations in the seventies and eighties is now narrowing fast.[8] The young are less radical; the old less reactionary. So there may be much less basis now for generation conflict, and no need for dogmas.

Where dogma can I suspect still be found though is among those hard-line political modernisers who have exploited differences in family values as a pretext for strengthening the role of the state in relation to ordinary families. It is their centralising reflex - which prefers to do things in the name of families, than to allow families the resources and rights to make their own choices within broadly agreed conventions - that is now beginning to look out of touch with the realities.

We should not be surprised at this. There have been several periods in the past when radical change in family life has been promoted, and manipulated, by political elites. But it is families, with older women in the vanguard, who end up defining the terms of eventual reconciliation between public and private lives. And it is with families as the leading partner, and state as their servant.[9]

Shortly after the last election I made the following observations:-

> *'This [neglect of the 'private realm' of family life] is arguably the single most important factor behind current alienation of ordinary people from politicians, ... Ironic as it may seem in the light of Labour Party performance and its closeness to the modernising movement, many older women appear to have voted Labour in 1997 in despair at the continuing failure of the Conservatives to come up with measures to match their pro-family rhetoric. ...*
> *Older women are a large and growing sector of the electorate. In 1992 they kept the Conservatives in power against the pollsters' predictions. Most are probably by nature more in tune with Tory world-views, and this more than anything probably accounts for Labour's long exile in the wilderness. If Labour is to have any hope at all of keeping their vote at the next election it will need to re-examine its attitude in government towards the private realm.'* [10]

These remarks are becoming ever more pertinent, as New Labour starts to run out of goodwill. The choice moreover is fairly simple. A government which neglects to listen to grandmothers, and regards *them* as stuck in the past, does not itself deserve and cannot expect to have much of a future.

VETERAN GRANDMOTHERS

CALLING ALL GRANDPARENTS

Erin Pizzey

A CHILDHOOD WITHOUT GRANDPARENTS

I grew up with a very dysfunctional mother and father. The one thing they did agree about unanimously was their dislike for each other's parents. According to my mother, my paternal grandmother was a 'prostitute' who married my violent and alcoholic Irish grandfather and bore him seventeen children. My paternal grandfather was one of the first policemen to pound the pavements in Brentford when he was sober and to race his horses when he was not. He was an enormous, intimidating man, but my father had fond memories of dancing on the bar of *The Black Lion* public house in Hounslow to entertain the customers when he was three years old. The eldest brother 'Jack' raced the horses when things were flush and then all of the boys delivered coal with the same horses when they were bust.

My father hated his mother and refused to talk about her. My mother insisted that my grandmother died in a mental

Erin Pizzey is a pioneering campaigner for the interests of women and children, and founded the first Shelter for Battered Wives *in Britain, at Chiswick, in 1971. She has written several novels and a number of books on human relations, starting with* Scream quietly or the neighbours will hear, *and most recently* The wicked world of women. *She has one son, five foster sons and one daughter. Since this chapter was written, her grandson Keita, who was diagnosed as a paranoid schizophrenic, has committed suicide in Wandsworth Prison.*[11]

hospital. She weighed eighteen stone and, according to my mother, I was 'just like her'.

My father insisted that my maternal grandmother died of TB in a sanatorium in Switzerland when my mother was two years old, leaving my maternal grandfather with three very young children. Whatever the truth of the matter, family documents show that he married a Miss Shaw, and that they left Ireland to make their lives in Canada. When my maternal grandmother died, my grandfather remarried and gave his two daughters away to remote relatives. This grandfather was also a violent alcoholic. When I was a small child I met him in Canada for a few hours, where his exploits were legendary. He wrote letters and legal documents for the surrounding neighbours, and he built most of the barns and houses in his surrounding area. He is reputed to have died falling off a wall he was building at the age of ninety-one.

It is no wonder that with such a colourful family background I wished I had been fortunate enough to know them all. I grew up, like so many children in those days of Colonial imperialism, in the servants' quarters wherever my bully of a father was posted. I learned very early that I could escape the worst of my mother's blows by running into the arms of the various cooks that lived with us in different countries in the Middle East. It was here that I think I got my deep understanding of the value of an extended family life.

Information about my own grandparents was almost impossible to come by. I fantasised during the long, lonely years when I was at boarding school in England, and my parents were abroad, that somewhere I had grandparents of my own. In fact both sets of grandparents were dead, but I made a childish vow to myself that one day I would be a grandmother and I would be able to be close to my grandchildren.

I envied other children at school and at my holiday home who had grandparents who would take them out and, even better, take them home for a visit.

ROLLING UP MY SLEEVES

I was thirty-seven when I first discovered that I was going to
be a grandmother. Nobody was more surprised than my
daughter and her boyfriend. They insisted that they did not
have full sexual intercourse, and I believed them. My daughter
often had irregular periods and so, apart from being tired, she
had no reason to suspect she was pregnant until she felt my
grandson move within her. She was pregnant and I laughed
when I felt my grandson kicking against my hand. There was
no point in remonstrating with my frightened fourteen-year-old
daughter. She was nearly seven months pregnant and it was
time to comfort and support a young girl who was still a child
herself.

I refused to listen to the war chants of other women. My
daughter wanted her child. She never for one moment thought
about putting my grandchild up for adoption. I stood looking
down at his huge brown eyes and thinking to myself that he
was not only a surprise but also a much-welcomed addition to
my huge family. Keita grew up with his mother and his father
in my house. I also had my son Amos and several other
'fostered' boys. Of course it was sometimes very difficult. Both
Keita's parents were very young. His father was struggling to
begin his career as a musician. The house rocked with loud
music and various friends. I ran the refuge by day and came
home to cook gigantic meals for all the children and then drop
into bed exhausted.

I had to take full financial responsibility for my daughter
and her family. I never resented having to do this. I felt very
privileged to be able to be that close to my grandson. He was
an enchanting little boy. His exuberance filled the house. From
a very early age he played on the various guitars that lay
around the house. He was not only musically gifted but he also
loved to draw and to paint. However, with the experience I
gained from taking in some thousand mothers and children a
year at my Chiswick refuge, I recognised that he was a very

emotionally and physically fragile child. He was ill a lot. He grew very thin under any stress, and he bonded very closely to his father.

My grand-daughter was born eighteen months later. She arrived in spite of a carefully fitted contraceptive coil. Unlike my grandson, she was a big strong little girl. She looked very like a sumo wrestler. I had no worries about her vulnerability. This time various people around the family had demanded that I bully my daughter into an abortion. My position on abortion has always been that whilst I religiously would never consider an abortion myself, I respected the right of other women to make their own choices. My daughter did not want an abortion and as I would, yet again, be the only adult to take financial responsibility for her choice, I told her to make her decision and I would stand by her. This time there was wide criticism but I was glad she chose to have my grand-daughter. The magazine *Private Eye* chose to refer to my grandchildren as 'bastards' and to speculate about my fitness to run the refuge. I preferred to ignore their attack.

I think of my years as a very young mother - I was twenty-one when I gave birth to my daughter - and then a very young grandmother as years shrouded by exhaustion. However, because my own children were now teenagers, I recaptured some of the magic of early childhood. I was young enough and confident enough to work all day and then sit up all night writing for *Cosmopolitan* and other periodicals to keep the food on the table. The house was shabby and capacious and I was happy with my extended family.

I was very aware that my daughter lost much of her teenage years. What I tried to do sometimes, without success, was to try to see that she had a life outside her children. She was forced to leave school because of her pregnancy, and fortunately our house was full of books and music. But even then, much of the time she was exhausted. I could only look upon her situation and hurt for her. The father of the children soon founded a rock group and began to move away. This was hardly surprising but still caused great stress in our family. I had always imagined that my role as a grandmother would be to float into my daughter's house and spoil my grandchildren rotten. The reality of my life as a grandmother was that I had to roll up my sleeves and pitch in.

So passionate was I, and so grateful to be a grandmother, that I rather overlooked the fact that I was called 'grandma' under the age of forty. Many of my women friends were appalled at the idea of being grandmothers when their time came and many insisted that they would not allow their grandchildren to call them grandma. I revelled in the title. I suppose that my almost orphaned existence meant that family life was precious to me. I know that I was horrified at the disintegration of family life around me and the carelessness with which so many of my feminist contemporaries dismissed the role of grandparents in their children's lives.

REBUILDING THE EXTENDED FAMILY

In my work at the Chiswick refuge, I made a point of encouraging the mothers to contact any members of their family they felt could contribute to the stability of their children's lives. When I travelled in order to lecture, I also made a point of contacting grandparents' groups to talk to them about the need to get laws changed to give grandparents rights to access to their grandchildren. Becoming a grandmother reinforced my sense of the generational value of family life. At night my daughter and I often sat together with her children and I marvelled at the sense of continuity the grandchildrens' presence gave me.

I think the first time I held my firstborn grandson in my arms and looked down at his huge brown eyes I felt an awesome sense of my own immortality. I was holding my child's child. Your grandchildren don't belong to you, they belong to their own parents. So the role of a grandparent is necessarily a very delicate one. For most grandparents the difficulties are mostly unthreatening but for some, I knew by now, the role of grandparent can become an absolute nightmare.

Most grandparents dream about having their grandchildren as a huge bonus and a reward for the years of deprivation and struggle bringing up their own children. The relationship you have with your grandchildren is normally far more relaxed. Grandparents should play the same role in the family as an elder statesman can in the government of a country. They have the experience and knowledge that comes from surviving a great many years of life's battles and the wisdom, hopefully, to recognise how their grandchildren can benefit from this. They can offer their grandchildren time and patience that is often in short supply in the arduous years of parenting. The time your grandchildren spend with you is a bonus for both sides. You know that however exhausting your grandchildren are they are still the primary responsibility of their parents, and they will be returned.

I lived for seven years in Santa Fe, New Mexico, where I ran a refuge and worked on child abuse cases and prosecuted paedophiles. Working within the multi-cultural community there I was aware of the Hispanic tradition whereby grandparents still played an essential part in their grandchildren's lives and saw that in the American Indian community too family life was still thriving. Most of the child abuse and sexual abuse in my cases came from within the Anglo community, where there were no family links. The children were open to sexual predators, and it was here where I discovered the prevalence of female sexual abuse.

In the early days the feminist movement's revolutionary slogan was 'from the personal to the political'. In too many cases what this meant was that women who came from violent and dysfunctional families found themselves as leaders of the women's movement in the Western world. I was greatly influenced by Leo Tolstoy's remark that, "All happy families resemble one another, but each unhappy family is unhappy in its own way."[12] I could see the generational violence in my own life. I was aware that my mother was never mothered, and that when I had my daughter my greatest source of insecurity was that I had no mother to consult. Apart from the fact that my mother was violent and dysfunctional, she had died when I was seventeen. My experiences within the confines of my own violent family life made me determined that I would make notes of the happy, normal families that surrounded me and that I would try to emulate the mothers in those families. I saw clearly that the problem lay within the abnormal violent family members, contaminated by the generational violence in their own families, who then spread their condemnation of *all* family life into their personal and political life.

CYCLES OF VIOLENCE

I recognised this generational violence in the case histories that I compiled with each mother coming into my refuge with her children. I could trace the violence back several generations, and what interested me was that when the violence was passed down from the *maternal* side of the family it resulted in the women who came into Chiswick being violent themselves. Where the grandmothers were violent both physically and emotionally to their daughters and their sons, the girls in the family were more likely to be violent towards their own children than if it was the grandfathers who were violent.

This was not always obvious. 'Ida' for example was a grandmother in her late seventies who brought her small grandson in because she feared that her son was going to harm him. Her son was very violent, and Ida confessed that her life with her husband had been extremely violent. We managed to rescue the boy from his father's violence. But Ida herself died from the effects of a kicking inflicted on her by this son. I was already conscious of banner headlines in newspapers talking about 'battered elderly parents'. The journalists seemed to think that abnormal children were turning upon their elderly parents, and that this was a new phenomena. What they could *not* see was that battered and abused children were turning back on their abusive parents when the parents were too old to inflict the violence upon them.

I opened my refuge at the time of Sir Keith Joseph's remark that he saw a 'cycle of depravation' within problem families. As I said at the time, I too saw a 'cycle of generational violence within violence-prone families'. Very quickly I sought to develop a therapeutic community setting for the many violent women who came into the refuge with their children. I tried to recreate family life, and from the beginning I found both male and female staff to work in the refuge who could act as surrogate mothers, grandmothers, aunts and uncles to the families.

One of the most important women in our community was Phil Pepper, who was in her sixties when she came to work in the community. Phil was the ideal grandmother for the refuge community - a woman of huge energy, great authority and a wicked sense of humour. Whenever possible we contacted grandparents of the families and often, when the relationship was fraught within the families, we worked to heal the breaches. Family life was all-important to the therapeutic idea at Chiswick. Even if the fathers were violent - and many of them had criminal records - where at all possible we helped to keep them in contact with their children.

THE HEALING POWER OF GENERATION

Many times I discovered when I contacted the grandparents that even if they had been violent towards their own children, they were only too happy to learn new ways of relating to their own grandchildren. Age mellows much aggressive behaviour. When the mothers learned to transcend their own violence they often made their way back to their own parents, allowing them to make relationships with their grandchildren where they had failed with their own children.

Many of the mothers came from institutional care where they had no parenting. Many were not only physically abused but also sexually abused by the staff who were supposed to care for them. When I first opened the refuge I was told that the work that I was doing was pointless because the women coming in would probably return to their violent relationships. Sixty-two of the first hundred women that came to Chiswick were from violent families themselves. It was no surprise to me that they returned to their dysfunctional and violent relationships. I discovered that 'violence-prone women', women who were from violent parenting themselves, were victims of their own violent childhoods and sought other violent relationships. It was being unable to turn to their own dysfunctional parents or grandparents which made them so vulnerable. 'Battered women' on the other hand, that is women who were victims of their *partners'* violence, *were* able to make the break from these violent partners, because violence was not a natural part of their own experience of relationships. They often could return to their parents' or grandparents' houses, because their families were still intact and could function as a refuge.

Because the feminist movement launched such a rabid attack upon family life in this country, they succeeded in creating policies that separated the extended family until the only unit left was that of the mother and her children. Grandparents had no rights to see their children, or to pass on the wisdom and the sense of family history that comes with grandparenting. The father's role likewise was rendered expendable. Men and boys generally became suspect in family life, and the feminists pursued various campaigns insisting that all men were guilty of rape and battery by virtue of being born male.

As the feminisation of our society crept into the schools and across academia, men moved out of teaching and caring roles and - aware of the slurs and of the dangers of being near children - retired from the front line of child care. Fathers and grandparents lost access to their children and grandchildren through divorces. Many of the violence-prone women who managed to use the court system against their husbands and partners also then barred the paternal grandparents from seeing their grandchildren.

Violence-prone women cannot see that grandparents have anything to offer their children. One of the hallmarks of a violence-prone personality is morbid jealousy, and any attempt from the grandparents or the father to contact the children will result in the mother feeling violently and abusively threatened.

Many grandfathers that I have known, especially in Canada and America, have been traumatised by a daughter-in-law's accusation that they have sexually molested their grandchildren. For a violence-prone woman this is the easiest way of ridding herself of the unwanted attentions of a grandparent. The grief and the suffering caused by many of the unfounded allegations made by disturbed daughters-in-law has led both grandmothers and grandfathers quite literally to die before their time. The burden of proving their innocence is left to the grandparents. The mother's accusations, even if they are proved to be false, go unpunished.

There are now moves internationally by grandparents' groups to fight for legislation giving them the right to remain in their grandchildren's lives. In my opinion, the role of grandparents is far too vital to allow them to remain ignored and excluded. The damage done to families by the feminist movement, in so many countries, is now beginning to alarm some policy-makers. Our own government is trying to make legislation more family-friendly, and our fathers' groups are beginning to grow more confident and capable. Greater recognition of the importance of grandparenting, and legal support to see that grandparents are able to play a role in their grandchildren's lives, are vital to the resuscitation of the family.

It is time for grandparents to come out of the cold.

Watching the Family Unfold

Senga Brealey

When I reflect on my family history I realise just how much continuity there is in it even though the lives of my grandchildren are very different from those of their forefathers. There have been many changes in the world, and I worry about the future. But in some ways, inside the family, things seem quite similar.

Memories of Childhood

I was born into a household consisting of my mother, father, twin brothers five years my senior and my maternal grandmother. It was not until much later in my life that I realised that my Grannie, who had been born, bred and lived all her life in Edinburgh, had been left almost destitute on the death of her husband. My father had been captain on a hospital ship based in Bombay during the first world war, and my mother was with him there. When they returned to this country and set up home in the London area, Grannie came to live with them.

I remember Grannie as a very old lady. She dressed in black, and her gowns were to the floor. She always wore long

Senga Brealey is a widow living by herself in a London suburb. During the war she served in the WRNS in Sri Lanka; but since then she has not had paid employment. She has two sons and a daughter, and nine grandchildren ranging in age from five to twenty.

sleeves and her outdoor wear consisted of a long black coat, black gloves and a hat (slightly reminiscent of a Queen Mary's toque) in black, with a veil or net which tied under her chin. I remember her as being very quietly spoken, very gentle and when I got into trouble I would be comforted by her. Looking back I realise now that she had very little social life as she had no friends in the area, and her outings were just to the butchers and to a little sweet shop and at both those places she would go into a back room and have a cup of tea with the shop-keeper's wife. As we had two maids to do the housework Grannie did most of the cooking.

Grannie had her own bedroom which consisted of a double bed - and I remember a lovely brass bedstead with large brass knobs which fascinated me - a washstand with marble top, a dressing table, wardrobe and large cupboard. She also had an easy chair, but Grannie was always with us - or is that just a memory? We were not allowed to wander into her bedroom and could never go in when she was not there.

She was brought up as a Presbyterian, but never attended church. However the Minister did come quite often to the house. But as we knew the family very well, and I was at school with his daughter, did he come to see us or Grannie? She did a lot of sewing and knitting but never on Sunday, when she also objected (in a very quiet way) to the playing of cards by any member of the family.

On occasion she would act as a buffer between my mother and myself, and I clearly remember asking her first if I could have friends round for tea - mainly because she used to make us lovely sandwiches. My parents went out most Saturday evenings and I was then left with my Gran. I remember playing card games and board games and of course always staying up later than the stipulated time for going to bed.

Every year Grannie would catch a cold and take to her bed for about two weeks. This became a family joke and it was always said she needed 'spoiling'. Then one October she took to her bed and the doctor was duly called, and he said that nothing was wrong with her but she needed fussing. I remember coming home from school one afternoon and going up to see her, and she was sitting up in bed. Mother then asked me to go up to the shops and I clearly remember Grannie saying that she would like to die as she had lived a long and good life and felt very happy and content. Mother was horrified, and her reply was, "Don't you dare die as flowers are very expensive in October." Yes, we all laughed.

I went to the shops, probably away for half an hour, and when I returned my beloved Grannie was dead. Her body remained in the bedroom for possibly one or two days and then the coffin was placed on trestles in the lounge. Neighbours came in to pay their last respects and I remember everybody trying to persuade me to see my Grannie as apparently she looked beautiful and like a young bride. But I suppose I was frightened. The funeral service was held in the lounge, conducted by the Minister who knew her.

My paternal grandparents lived in Edinburgh, and I saw them twice a year. They came down to London and stayed with us for two weeks in the Summer, and my parents returned to Edinburgh for a fortnight every October and when I was young I went with them. After a certain age I would travel to Edinburgh with my maternal grandmother, who went there for a month every year. We were met at Waverley station by my paternal uncle, aunt and a cousin my own age. I stayed with them while Grannie would go to stay with her sister, and then meet me for the journey back to London. I remember the train journeys, as we always had two booked window seats, and the high spot was going into the Restaurant Car for lunch.

During my visit, my cousin and I always had to stay with the paternal grandparents for a few days, and I remember that if our stay was over a weekend we dreaded Sunday. My grandparents were strict Episcopalians, and that meant no whistling, no ball games, in fact no games at all, no knitting etc, and our outing was to the Botanical Gardens where we had to walk very ladylike and always dressed in hat and gloves.

My grandparents went for lunch twice a week to Crawfords Restaurant, Princes Street, where they had a booked table so were greeted by name. When staying with them with my parents I remember having to be on my very best behaviour. Grandmother was always nicely dressed, and I can picture her now ready to go out, complete with hat, gloves and long umbrella. To read the menu, grandmother used a lorgnette mounted on a long gold handle and I was fascinated by it. Grandfather of course had a silver-topped walking stick. Oh happy days, and quite another way of life! I don't recall ever being hugged by my paternal grandmother, and perhaps she was as afraid of me as I was of her. I was certainly afraid of my grandfather when I was young, though when I went back to visit him when I was in my twenties I found him a very loving old man.

BECOMING A PARENT

When my first two children were born, one boy and one girl, my husband and I were living in Rugby. On both occasions while I was in the nursing home my parents travelled from London and took over the running of the house. My second son was born when we had returned to London and owned our own house but within easy distance of my parents. When he was born my husband was abroad for three months, and for that period I lived with my parents. I was quite ill before the birth, confined to bed so my parents did everything for the two little ones - one not yet four and the other not yet two.

Probably this close contact did form a special relationship between my children and their maternal grandparents. My children were always very close to their grandparents, and it was my father, 'Bampa' to them, who would take them for walks in the park and play with them. They were accustomed to being left in their charge, and if I made a fuss about leaving them or delayed going it was one of the children who would say, "Why don't you just go". My parents came for tea twice a week so on those occasions it would be Bampa who fetched them from school. And as we were members of a tennis club, we would be together most weekends.

My daughter can remember when she was around the age of eleven, walking on her own to visit my parents, and the reason was to have tea with her Grannie. This was probably during school holidays, and also every Friday we would go to my parents' home for tea as the children went to Scottish dancing in a hall nearby.

The other grandparents, my husband's parents, did not have such a close relationship with the children. They lived in Derby and came down for a fortnight every summer, and every Christmas. And we paid frequent visits to them. As the children got older - I think from the age of about five - each in turn went to stay with their paternal grandparents for a fortnight in the summer holiday.

When my father died my mother, then aged eighty, came to live with us but she had her own bedroom and sitting room. By that time two of the grandchildren were at university and the youngest was in the sixth form. My mother lived with us until she died aged ninety-eight - and still a very healthy old lady with all her wits about her. I don't think the children considered her to be an 'old lady' in the same way as I remember my Grannie.

A GRANNIE MYSELF

I think that there is some similarity in the relationship between my Grannie and my mother, myself and my mother, and my daughter and myself. In a way we are quite a close family all round.

Although I get on very well with my two daughters-in-law and love them dearly, I do feel that my relationship with my daughter is a very special one. She was married, but unfortunately this broke up after a serious operation when she was told she would never have a child. She formed another relationship, but her new partner made it clear from the beginning that he didn't want children and when she became pregnant, he left. End of story.

I saw my grandson Nicholas being born, so consider him to be 'mine'. She has brought her son up on her own and at the beginning I suppose she did get a lot of support from both her parents. As she lived with Nicholas in a two bedroom first-floor flat they came back to our home every weekend. She has a First Class Honours degree in Maths and worked in computers, but did not return to work after the birth of her son until he was five years old. During this time she studied in the mornings for two more 'A' levels at adult education classes while I looked after Nicholas. And when he started school she attended the Institute of Education where she obtained a B.Ed. Recently she took her MA and is now a Deputy Head.

My grandson has had no contact with his father, and my daughter has no idea where he is. She did inform his parents when the child was born, feeling that they had a right to know about their grandson. But there was no reply. My sons did not cause any difficulty during this period and were most supportive of their sister. All the children were frequent visitors to our house, and I don't think that the other grandchildren showed any surprise that Nicholas had his own bedroom. In our garden we had a climbing frame with kitten run, a separate slide, a swingboat and two swings. No wonder they all came!

It is difficult to describe the relationship between Nicholas and myself, as I have always been connected with his life. Every year my daughter has gone on a walking holiday with a friend from university days, and during that period I have looked after him. Even when he was eighteen I moved in last summer, and when my daughter went trekking in Nepal, over Christmas and New Year, I again took over the household. He was most caring towards his elderly grandmother and took great care to let me know where he could be found when away from home. Mind you, he wasn't often at home. He is a flight-sergeant in the Air Training Corps, and recently received the Duke of Edinburgh Gold Award - a well-adjusted young man, with univeristy on the horizon.

I think in the early years for Nicholas it was his grandfather who had the greatest influence, and certainly if my husband had lived long enough he would have had a great say in his schooling and future career. When Nicholas was four years old my husband explained to him Einstein's *Theory of Relativity*, and weekends were spent doing woodwork (he had his own toolbox with full set of tools) making model aeroplanes or experimenting with the chemistry set. Nicholas was very close to his grandfather (my husband), and on one occasion - when just a toddler - we heard his cousin asking him why he hadn't got a Dad. The reply was, "I don't need a Dad, I have a Grandpa." I think as a grandparent I came second. But that might have changed by now. I am still close to him and I think we get on very well. They live about twenty minutes walk from me.

Another great influence on Nicholas' life was his great-grandmother, affectionately known as GG, who lived with us but had her own separate rooms. When Nicholas was staying with us he could often be found in her room, where she would be story-telling. When my mother became very ill and it was obvious she was not going to recover and was confined to bed, Nicholas would go and sit by the bed and sing nursery rhymes and just chatter away - usually getting no reply. He was then three to four years old. It was also quite obvious that GG knew Nicholas was with her. She would open her eyes and smile, and she adored her great grandson and to this day Nicholas has happy memories of time spent with her.

It is my daughter's son that I am closest to. But with the other grandchildren I have had a lot of contact too. I have never had a job, so there was no problem when I looked after any of them and I did this fairly often for my eldest son's children when they lived near. When that grand-daughter was six and her brother four I looked after them for three weeks while their parents visited Australia. The maternal grandmother had care of the eighteen-month baby, and we all met up frequently to keep the family together. Although it may be a funny thing to say, the children did not seem to miss their parents, and my grand-daughter did say to her mother, on their return, that she would be quite happy to go and stay with Grannie again. This grand-daughter is now seventeen and I recently had the greatest pleasure of hearing her play oboe and piano in the final of the Maidstone and Mid Kent Young Musicians of the Year 2000, meaning another entry to university.

It is sad to say but I have not had so much contact with the youngest children of my younger son. His eldest son, now aged twenty, was a frequent visitor when he was a baby; and this continued more or less for the two who followed. But I have had little contact with the fourth and fifth children. We were more together all as a family when my husband was alive and we lived in a very large house. But it is partly my fault. My daughter-in-law works, as a health visitor, and I feel that their family weekends are precious and busy enough without the added burden of visits from me. But I have an open invitation to visit whenever I wish, and we do have frequent family reunions.

THE FUTURE

I don't think there is any doubt that the role of grannie has altered considerably over just three generations, though perhaps that may be the fault of grannie. I feel I live a much fuller life than that of my mother, and certainly my grandmother. I own a car and I belong to various organisations - so being a single person does not limit my horizons (for want of a better word). I do very often count my blessings.

I worry about my grandchildren and wonder what life has in store for them. My generation suffered a war and it was our hope that life would improve for all and that peace was not just a dream. In reality it is all very different. What worries me firstly about the future is work prospects. At one time you got settled in a job and were there until retirement. But that is not now the case. Jobs are no longer secure. Then again, at the end of university life the graduate is left with a large debt at the bank. I feel very strongly about youngsters having no grants to help with university costs.

Also I feel that discipline and respect is lacking among the young generation. When I hear about some of the behaviour of children at my daughter's school, I am appalled. When the word of a child is believed before that of the adult, and children are well aware of this, then something somewhere is clearly wrong.

Children today do not have the freedom even my children had - like going for a picnic in the forest with no adult, or even the freedom of going out at night. Where my son lives is in an unlit street, with no pavements and a long walk to the bus stop. This means transport has to be provided for all evening activities, and this must prove very restricting to a teenager. And how does one control the use of drugs; why do so many youngsters, specially girls, smoke; and why is pregnancy at such a young age on the increase?

I am sometimes told by my grandson, but in a very nice way, that I am old-fashioned. And yes, I guess I am. I wonder whether at some time he will think back and remember his grannie as a very old lady. I am glad I am not a youngster today as I feel my life has not had so much pressure, and if I had the chance to live my life all over again then there is very little I would wish to change.

THE LONG MARCH

Jean Stogdon

BREAKING OUT

The lives of women in my family have been going through a transformation for over a century. But the pace of change has become much more rapid in my own life-time than it was earlier on. In essence my maternal grandmother Catherine - born in 1877 in Wales - my mother Mary - born 1902 in Wales - and I - born 1928 in London - have all had the same goal as grandmothers. Despite our differing social, political and emotional experiences we have all been mothers, and then grandmothers involved in the care of our grandchildren.

I believe that we have been, as grandmothers, strong caregivers who tried (and in my case still try) to instill in our grandchildren a sense of humanity and an ability to prevail. They were role models for me, before the invention of the term. They taught me how to live and behave and care, and I attempt to be the same for my grandchildren.

But there have been important differences as well, and these arise from the way that their roles were limited and more clearly defined and constrained. Both Catherine and my mother

Since retiring from her job as a senior social worker, Jean Stogdon has played an active part in the development of organisations representing grandparents. During 2000 she visited grandparents' groups in US on a Winston Churchill Fellowship. *A former chair of the* Grandparents' Federation, *she is currently setting up a new group, with a broader scope embracing 'kinship care', to be known as* Grandparents Plus.

Mary were wives, mothers, grandmothers, aunts, sisters, nieces and cousins. But that is *all* they were or seemed to be. They had no other permitted identity beyond those familial ones. As I left school at fourteen in 1942, married at nineteen in 1948 and had three children in the 1950s, it was perhaps natural to think that I would also be confined to those roles.

In 1966 however an event occurred which changed my life forever, and led to a personal revolution which projected me out of the role of 'just a housewife'. I had a still-born baby, which ended prematurely my child bearing years and forced me to look beyond the role of full-time mother. And so I jumped the high wall which enclosed the world of marriage and motherhood and ventured into the wider world.

I knew that I was doing something unusual in the 1960s, in the suburbs, where none of my friends or neighbours went out to work. But I had no idea that in order to gain a separate professional identity outside the family I would have to go through so much anger and pain. Clearly in those days I had not heard of strategies to manage change. I was doing the unforgivable by stepping out of my appointed role. I chose social work; or maybe it chose me. Of the several older women on my course all divorced soon afterwards. That was the difference between Catherine, my mother and myself. They never threatened the status quo, or had the opportunity to do so, except by maverick unsanctioned acts with the risk of ostracism and shame.

MY GRANDMOTHER'S LIFE

Catherine's life had been cruelly hard, yet my mother told me she was gentle, warm and kind. It is said that Catherine died at the age fifty-two of hard work; certainly she had little of her life to call her own.

I was born nine months before she died; my mother took me to see her once before she died. I have always treasured the fact that she saw me. In quite a primitive way I have always felt close, and identified with her. I feel a thread running from her, through my mother and me to my granddaughters Hannah, Grace and Molly, although of course they have other influences too and other progenitors. I feel Catherine's influence to this day.

She was born in a remote village on the Llyn Peninsula in North Wales. It is said she was born in the same hour as her own grandmother died. She married James and had three daughters followed by five sons; my mother was the second oldest daughter. James was a labourer and the family lived from hand-to-mouth. James died in 1918 aged forty-three. There were no widows' pensions or allowances. In that rural poverty everybody's biggest fear was the workhouse; it was a reality for many people. Catherine was fortunate enough not to live in a tied cottage when James died otherwise the family would have been evicted. As it was my mother told me that James' sisters came and claimed the furniture after his death. Catherine sent my mother and one of her brothers up into the mountain with saucepans and other essentials of everyday living until after the sisters left.

The girls in the family were sent away at age thirteen to be live-in servants in the big houses in the cities; my mother went to Sheffield. The boys were sent to the big farms at the age of twelve and also lived in. When she was eighteen my mother became pregnant. This was not unusual; 'service' had connotations other than domestic work, with the male members of the household. For a year my mother was able to be with her daughter Mair in a mother and baby home, working there as a domestic, but after a year she had to leave to earn her living. She found a foster mother for Mair but on one of her visits my mother discovered they were ill-treating her. She told her mother Catherine. Her response was what grandmothers have done through the ages when there was no alternative, she said, "Bring her home, I will bring her up."

The year was 1923. Catherine had had her last child in 1915, she had been a widow for five years and had only six years to live. Catherine raised Mair, my half sister for six years until she could be reunited with her mother, my mother, when she married my father.

THE GENERATION OF SURVIVAL

I became really interested in Catherine's life as I peered through the window of a two-hundred-year-old stone crog-loft cottage several years ago. This was where Catherine had been born. She was to move to a similar crog-loft cottage when she married James. How could a family of ten people live in a single story cottage that looked like a gingerbread house with a central door and a sash window on either side? One window was in the parents' bedroom - the only bedroom - and the other was in the only living room. I can visualise it with an open fire with trivets - holding a large black cast iron saucepan on one and a huge black kettle on the other. There would have been a slate floor and simple table and benches. An important piece of furniture at the time was a *Cwpwrddgwydyr* (glass fronted cupboard) to hold all the families treasures; a souvenir cup brought back by a relative from a day trip to Llandudno; a birthday card, sepia with roses; a silk card sent back by a soldier from the trenches in France; a piece of Victorian cranberry glass.

The cottage was lit by oil lamp and candles in the bedroom. On the side of the room was a tall single ladder that went up to the crog loft, where all the children would sleep on their mattresses on the floor, plus any visitors or lodgers. A census I looked up revealed twelve people sleeping in the cottage one night. All cooking would be done on the open fire. A large black saucepan would hold *Lobscows*, a sort of stew consisting of a small piece of bacon from their own pig, cabbage and potatoes. A small oven alongside, heated by the fire, would bake the *Bara Brith*, a fruit loaf for special occasions. The kettle would perpetually 'sing', ready to offer a cup of tea for any visitor who came through the ever open door.

There would have been an outside pump for water and a bucket in a small shed at the end of the garden which was the lavatory. On one side of the cottage would be a cowshed and a pigsty. The butter would be churned from the milk and sold, as were the eggs from the chickens. The residue from the butter was buttermilk which, mashed with potatoes, was a staple in the family diet and was called *Tatwsllaith*. My mother asked for buttermilk when she was dying. As I looked through that crog loft window I longed to know about the detail of Catherine's life and indeed her mother's life. What happened to her in an ordinary day? What did she wear? How did she give birth? How had she managed to raise all those children to be decent human beings against all the odds? What was James like as a husband?

I know that statistically Catherine would have lost children between those that survived. I know she would have given birth at home and that birthing was 'women's business', with neighbours, friends and relatives all contributing.

I know that death was part of life. Death happened at home and was managed by families. At a recent funeral I attended in the same area there was a noticeable absence of professionals. The coffin was carried by male relatives who walked from the chapel to the cemetery.

Sex, birth, death, poverty, work, love and chapel were the elements of Catherine's life. One word describes it - survival.

THE GENERATION OF LOSS

My parents' home, mine until I married at nineteen and theirs from 1935 until 1982 and 1985 respectively was a small two up two down Victorian terrace in New Southgate, London with an outside lavatory. A bathroom was fitted in 1968. Both my grandmother and my mother spent the best part of Monday doing the washing. If it could not be dried outside it would have been hung about wet indoors. If there was one item in my life that contributed to my liberation more than any other it was the washing machine. Although I have lived in a good three bedroomed house from 1955 to date, I did not have a washing machine until my youngest son was born in 1959. It wasn't until 1969 that I had an automatic washing machine. It was that and my mother's help which enabled me to combine home and work.

Both my mother and my grandmother gave birth at home. I was a 10lb baby; the birth was difficult but there were very few caesarian sections in 1928. Neither my grandmother, my mother or myself had fathers present at the births, although in 1951 when I had my first child it was beginning to happen. I had all my children in hospital with a great deal of intervention.

A most vital factor in all our lives was health. My mother told me the village barber extracted teeth and even took out tonsils; people of that class would hardly have seen a doctor. Throughout my childhood I was aware that the doctor cost three shillings and six-pence and was rarely visited. The National Health Service started in 1948, the year I married. My family has had wonderful health care for over fifty years, free from anxiety.

My mother became a housewife in 1927 when she married my father. She never worked outside the home except for a bit of 'charring'. Although I was raised during the 1930s Depression my father as a skilled engineer was never out of work. He was a proud man, one of eight children born to Victorian parents steeped in the work ethic. His mother stayed at home and raised the children and although the number of children in families had greatly reduced in the 1930s he would have thought himself a failure if his wife went out to work and usurped his role as a provider.

Therefore my mother, having brought up my sister, brother and myself, moved seamlessly from her role as a full-time mother to a full-time grandmother when I had my first child aged twenty two. I had not known my grandmother as she died so young but my children knew their four grandparents into adult life. My mother's life was her children and grandchildren. She was bonded to them and they adored her. My children were deeply affected by her death at the age of eighty two. She had been a significant and important person to them.

Despite the improved physical circumstances of my mother's life, one word I believe encapsulates her life. Loss. Loss of her daughter Mair's early childhood. Loss of another child to adoption - Catherine could not care for two grandchildren. Loss of three brothers at a young age through ill-health; loss of so many childhood friends through TB; loss of cousins killed in the 1914-1918 war; loss of her parents at so young an age. Ironically, her grandparents lived into old age.

THE GENERATION OF CHOICE

When I became a grandmother nineteen years ago, in 1981, I was a manager of two hundred staff in a very busy Inner London social services department. I worked very long hours and was almost unavailable as a child-care resource for my grandchildren. I felt very guilty as my grandchildren were variously cared for in day nurseries, with child-minders and nannies. I questioned whether my career was more important than caring for my grandchildren whilst their parents worked. With a great struggle I came to terms with the fact, as today's parents must, that we have choices. We live in different times.

That dilemma continues for many grandparents to this day. We have done our bit, even the double shift. Now we look forward to freedom from work and to a certain extent from family responsibilities. We have responsibilities to ourselves. We have thirty odd years extra life this century and are fitter. There are greater opportunities for older people. If one word sums up my life it is - choice.

If grandparents are not what they used to be neither is the task of being a grandparent; we are in transition. Family life has changed so dramatically in the past decade, with working parents and the divorce rate so high. There is great diversity and ostensibly many options; it seems everyone wants to define and redefine family life. Grandparents are in the eye of the storm of change. Both my grandmother's and my mother's marriages were terminated by death; my own marriage is fifty-two years old yet already one of my sons is divorced. Divorce is a family business with grandparents witnessing the painful process but being powerless to do anything but stand by and support.

We have been lucky. Having sons increases the risk of losing touch with or even being denied contact with our grandchildren. Fortunately our relationship with our grandchildren is valued and continues to grow, and if anything contact is even more frequent as we adopt and adapt to the role of babysitters.

THE PROBLEM OF CHOICE

There are many different issues for grandparents, depending on the circumstances of our children. Some people will become grandparents by adoption, or they may lose their grandchildren through adoption. Others will have grandchildren in lesbian or gay households and may have to come to terms with what was previously unthinkable. A few will have grandchildren subject to care proceedings because their grandchildren have been neglected or abused. Furthermore, grandchildren could have at least one parent from a different ethnic group. We may lose grandchildren through divorce or gain grandchildren and become step-grandparents. Our grandchildren's parents may be disabled, or the children may need special help. All these situations and many others are ripe for conflict.

Taking advantage of the greater opportunities for older people, at the age of seventy-one I was fortunate enough to travel to America on a Winston Churchill Fellowship to study grandparents. Four million grandparents there are raising their grandchildren, parenting again when they thought they were at last free of full child-care responsibilities.

Most grandparents will step in, as did Catherine with my mother, if needs must. But there is evidence that there may be ambivalence if we are asked to do too much, at a moment when we are poised to pursue our own choices and opportunities, perhaps for the first time after a life of work.

But love is deep and family continuity and family preservation are vitally important to most grandmothers. Although most of our caring is invisible and unsung I believe it is the glue that holds many families together. Stability and the extended family have never been needed more than now with the nuclear family under such stress.

A profound change, a revolution, has indeed occurred. My grandmother and mother were its quiet and determined and even unwitting authors. I have inherited their values, and must give voice to their achievements and re-create their example for today, and face today's problems. The march goes on.

STARTING ALL OVER AGAIN

Joyce Cottle

I always seem to have some of my grandchildren staying here with me. At the moment it's Hannah, who is fifteen, and her sister Ruth who is eighteen. It is partly to give my daughter Janice a bit of space. But it is also because Ruth is expecting in a few months. So I shall be a great-nan - and if my mother had lived just another year she would have been a *great*-great-nan! I'm excited about it because we'll have another baby in the family. And we love babies in this family, it's like starting all over again. I just love having grandchildren. The evenings I enjoy most of all, because I like to sit with them and I like to read them stories.

It is a bit inconvenient when there are several of them staying here at once. With Ruth it's only temporary; well it's meant to be, it could go on longer. It is inconvenient because after you've brought your own family up you want to have space to yourself. But I wouldn't want to see her lost. I've always said that I'm here for them if they need me. That's how it has been over the years.

I love having them up here even though my life is pretty busy. I work all day at the shop and then have my grandchildren after school. Then one day's over and then the next one comes and it goes on; very hectic. And come the weekends, one of my daughters has to work sometimes and

---

Joyce Cottle is a shop assistant living in West Hampstead. She is divorced with four children - who all live reasonably nearby - and seven grandchildren, two of whom are currently living with her.

when she does her son Danny comes up here. He would like to live with me really, but I would not let him. I say to him, "You've got to go home."

DANNY

Danny is the son of my middle daughter Joanne. She works full-time and doesn't live with his father - although Danny does see his dad quite a bit. He would love to live with me, but I have to say no because if he does there are others who would want to as well. Like Chelsea. She is fourteen and does not like it at home as there's two other little ones and always a lot of hullabaloo. She doesn't get any peace. She often comes up to my flat to wash her hair in peace, as she can't get into the bathroom at home. She's got lovely long hair, and she's a bit vain about it. She'll say something like, "Nan, we're all going out tonight and it means that I'm not going to get in the bathroom. Can I come up to yours and wash my hair?" I will say, "Yeah, by all means," and she will trot round to wash it.

Danny is nine and he'd love to live with me. He says, "Can I stay with you all the time?" And I say, "No Danny, you've got to go home." And then he goes on, "But I haven't slept with you for a long time." And I say, "But Danny, you shouldn't keep sleeping with me." I mean, he refuses to sleep in another room, he has to sleep in my bed. He sleeps on the furthest point from me, it is just that he likes my bed. I say to him, "Danny, you're going to be sleeping with your nan when you're eighteen!" We were laughing about it the other night. He said, "No I won't, I won't. I'll sleep in the other room." I don't know what it is, they just love being here.

He finds it easier being here with me than with his mum. He has been a very hyperactive child, and sometimes as soon as his mother walks through this front door he gets all agitated. He was the type of child who would hit his head on the wall. He has grown out of that now, but she had to take him to the psychiatrist to make sure that there was nothing wrong. They said that he is a nice little boy. He is. He's polite most of the time, but he has his moments when he plays up and he has to have the last word. I think that he's a bit spoilt now because he gets his own way a lot. He does what he likes. His dad always buys him playstations and those games. I think dads try to outdo mums sometimes when they're not together. They try to buy bigger presents.

I find that I get on very well with him. Joanna was forever shouting at him, and I said, "You don't have to shout at him like that!" But it was the only way she could get through to him, unless she smacked him. She's a single-parent mum. She goes to work full-time. She's got the pressures of home and she has to pay full rent, full this, full that - she doesn't get any help. I think it did all get on top of her. But she should start getting better now as she has just had a rise at work and some other little things that make her life a bit easier.

She never married Danny's father. They just never got on, though things are better now. She goes round for dinner sometimes, and I said to her last time, "I can see you getting back together someday." And she said, "I don't know. He's got a very bad temper; even the boy takes after him." Not that his temper does come out a lot. But you can see his dad in him.

OUT WITH DANNY

Danny is terrific out shopping, though. I can give him my shopping list and say to him, "Go and get me the teabags," and off he will go and bring them back. Little things like that. He's a great help. But I think that's because I take him out shopping, and she won't. I tell him he has to come with me, and I say to him, "Put the shopping in the trolley," and he packs it for me. Sometimes he pushes it all the way back from Tesco. It's quite a slog. If it was for his mum he wouldn't do it; he would probably run to the end of the road.

She is glad that we get on so well. There have been times when I've said to her that I can't have him any more because he's been so naughty. He gets so bored. Now he's got his toys here. He's got a playstation to put on the telly. He's got a big box of cars too. So that keeps him occupied. I think the world of him. I love him but it's not the same as your own child. He's got to go home sometimes. I wouldn't take him over completely. She's got to have him. I love him to stay if she is going out anywhere. And sometimes if I am in the right frame of mind I say, "Alright, he can stay." But most times he goes home.

Sometimes she goes to things straight after work and I say, "No, you've got to pick him up first, otherwise it can become too much of a habit!" I've brought up my family, and this is the next generation. I don't think it is fair that I should be responsible for him - which is what it sometimes feels like. I would have him for weekends while she went on a course for work, and I would be responsible for taking him to school and making sure that he came home and then feeding him. I don't mind doing it. But he has got a parent, and it's their responsibility.

I did take him on holiday too, with his other nan - his dad's mum. We all get on very well. We're a close-knit family and we took him to Minorca for a week. He was terrific. We only had two incidents with him when he got a bit stroppy, and we can handle him. Now he tells people, "I went away with nagging nans!" It was funny. But he loves us both and he's always telling us he loves us you know. And I don't know whether that means he is insecure when he keeps doing that. My grand-daughter of fourteen phones me up all the time and she always says, "I love you, Nan," at the end of the conversation. Its nice to hear them say it at times. But we never used to say anything like that when I was young.

THE WAY THINGS WERE

I don't think that I can have been as close to my nan as my grandchildren are to me. She always seemed very old, though she was only in her late sixties when she died. I vaguely remember *her* mother, but I must have been very young and she must have been in her late eighties when she died. My dad's parents I never saw, as they died before the war.

I can remember coming home from school and going to my nan's place. My mum used to work, so we always went into my gran's and had bread and jam. We had either bread and jam or bread pudding. When I was small it was the war years and just after. So my dad wasn't around and we lived with an aunt and my cousin, next door to my gran, and my cousin's dad wasn't around either. So our growing up years were all about the family.

My cousins lived in my house with me, and my aunt lived in my nan's house. But we had a communal back garden and we used to walk round the back way so there was no need to be coming out of the street door. There used to be a shelter in the garden. We used to go in my nan's because it was the nicest. It was all kitted out with bunk beds and things, so we used to go in there. But I can remember my nan had in her kitchen a really big, solid wooden table, and I can remember thinking if we had a really bad air raid we would all go under the table in the kitchen.

I can remember having a bath in there too. Friday night was bath night round at nan's house, and they'd put up this great big bath and take it in turns. It wasn't until we were teenagers that we started going down the local baths. When you're tiny you're too young to do that. We went down there a couple of times a week. We used to have a relative who worked down there, and she used to give us all lovely hot water. You took your own soap and towel, and we used to put soda in.

When I first got married we took over the top front room in my nan's house. For two or three years we lived in one room. My nan had died by then, but I still had an uncle in the house. Why we ever took it I don't know. You'd never take anything like that in this day and age. There was an outside loo, and we used to have to put a penny in the gas meter for the cooker which was in the scullery where we used to do the washing. If we had taken a photo of our room, people would say how comfortable it looked, as we had a big fireplace with an open coal fire. But it was so cold in there. It was horrible. But mum lived next door, so we spent half the time there.

My mum had the luxury of inside water as well. The kids of today don't know what luxury they live in. There's no outside loo or having to go to the baths. Our lives changed a lot once we moved out of the old houses. They were slums. And we were slum kids. I have only had central heating for about seven years now, and I never thought that I would get used to it.

Family life is very different these days, mainly because people just live together. It isn't that there is more divorce. There are fewer people getting married. And maybe that puts greater pressure on grandparents. But what I've found is that it all evens out in the end. My daughter had an unhappy relationship, and I said I'd always help out. And it all evened out and the pressure wasn't too much. I'm always here for the children. That's my experience. How it works for other people I don't know.

WHAT REVOLUTION: WHOSE REVOLUTION?

Fay Weldon

THE VANISHING CHILDREN

I have four grandchildren. A boy of seventeen, and his brother of thirteen via son number one, now in his forties. A step-grandson of eight and a grand-daughter of five from son number two in his thirties. There are two sons to go, so far childless. The likelihood of the younger two having children diminishes annually, as the birth rate falls and young professional women, wives and partners are less and less inclined to have children.

Thus my mother, now over ninety, having had two daughters, has seven grandchildren and ten great grandchildren. But I doubt that in the next generation down she will muster as many.

Such an exponential growth, some might say, is just as well curtailed – but as the proportion of women who marry and have children diminishes from its peak in the mid-fifties, the overall birth rate is well below the replacement level – 1.8 instead of the desired 2.0 – and is falling fast. Good for world resources, I daresay, but already a source of grief to friends of

Fay Weldon has written numerous television plays, dramatisations and stage plays. Her novels include Down Among the Women, The Hearts and Lives of Men *and* Life and Loves of a She Devil. *She has been chairperson of the* Booker Prize *judges. Her work has been translated into most main world languages. She lives and works in London, and is married with four sons and four grandchildren.*

mine in their sixties, who strike their heads and cry, "But where are my grandchildren?"

Where indeed – sacrificed to the need of the ergonarchy, the rule by the work ethic, in which women are out to work, and one wage is no longer enough to support a group of dependants. The erstwhile role of the male as maintainer of the family is increasingly taken over by the state in the form of family credit, sole parent benefits and so on; and the role of the erstwhile female as child-carer likewise, by the state as represented by the school. The 'school' now takes children from the age of three, until well into adulthood, for training and conditioning the better to slip them into a gender-free workforce. School hours shift to fit in with office hours, where once the hope was that it would be the other way round.

It may seem to the grandparent that today's society is given a sense of national cohesion by its common fears, rather than its aspirations: while my children came rushing shrieking from the school gate to peel off to their separate houses and a stay-at-home mother, my grandchildren and their friends cower inside for fear of strangers, until delivered one by one into the hands of a named collector. Yet the danger from the stranger is statistically no greater than it was fifty years ago.

My daughters-in-law live in acute anxiety during their early to mid-pregnancies – scans and amniocentesis make sure they do – as they wait for results which are seldom conclusive, but merely agitate and upset. The more we try to allay our fears, the more we reinforce them. This is about the only grandmotherly wisdom I can offer. Blind courage is preferable to sensible fear.

LIFE UNDER SHIFTING RULES

You may well ask me what part grandparenting plays in my own life. The only answer can be, it depends. I am still working and earning, as are many women in their fifties, sixties, even seventies. Grandparenting is like morality: what can be afforded, in terms of time, energy and money, and what can be afforded shifts and changes. The grandmotherly bond is not hard-wired into us, as some Darwinists would claim, unlike the maternal bond. Thanks to medicine and science we outlive nature's use for us, that's all – society may need us, and our friends, and indeed our grandchildren, but the acute anxiety which typifies the mother-child bond is on the whole absent in the grandparent, and thank God for that.

Grandmothering (for me at any rate) is a matter of propinquity, family connection and affection – not of 'bonding', which goes on between mother and child, the fierce and anxious protectiveness the former has to the latter, that lifetime sentence. I suspect the bond may be stronger when it progresses from daughter to grand-daughter, (the mitochondrial link, we could call it), than when it passes through sons. The affection between grandparent and grandchild flows with acquaintance.

It is hard to say what grandmothers should do or be like these days. The family is in such a state of flux it is hardly possible to lay down rules. Nice if they can baby-sit, if they can refrain from criticising. You could tell tales of life before the washing-machine, or more latterly, the microwave, of idyllic times when mother stayed at home, which is all the child wants, the better to resist it. (Children are not reasonable: passionate about their own survival – draining the mother of life and energy in order to establish their own.) Families split and reform. Grandparents can spread help and affection to ease the passage of the stepchild from the splitting home to the next household, which parents often quite forget to do, so absorbed are they by their own predicament. If allowed, grandmothers can frequently ice birthday cakes so they don't have to be bought from the shop: I suppose they could teach this skill, but to ask the grandchild to teach the grandparent computer games would be more to the point.

It is even harder to say *whose* revolution this all is. There are not really any rules any more. So it is no longer possible to identify a generational *position*, or even to determine a generation to which one belongs. So what is one to rebel against? Or whom with? My ideas reflect my own nature, rather than a spirit of the age. How to define that spirit anyway? The sixties were the generation of permissiveness, but I am not likely, post-Aids, to encourage my grandchildren towards sexual experimentation. Grandfathers regard their grandsons and their tender sensibilities in amazement, and give them condoms when they go abroad, which the grandsons give back, offended. Gender roles have switched, the older generation observe. The boys are the sensitive ones; it's the girls who are predatory. My generation was politically active and rioted in the streets – the grandchildren's generation have teachers who pride themselves on being *therapists too*, and end up interested in themselves rather than society.

So where is the pattern in this? Some people may think of grandparents as being in pinnies, baking scones, or pottering in the garden. Would that it were so. My mother supported her family. You have to go back to my grandmother – born 1882 – to find a traditional woman in this family who stayed home, and even she played the piano six hours every day and was a thwarted concert pianist. She lived with us when I was a child and read one detective story a day – if supply allowed – and passed them on to me. That was her contribution, and a fine one too.

My own experience, and my own values, are the same as those of many other people these days. One's own family life changes at the same rate as the rest of society's. There is a great deal of generational crossover too. I live with three step-sons in their teens all younger than my eldest grandchild. I don't think my values change, other than that once I thought it was vaguely unnatural for women to decide not to have children – now I most heartily recommend them not to. What a mother can do for a daughter, I daresay, is to make having the grandchild a possibility, in order that family genes have somewhere new to go.

DIARY OF A SUPERGRAN

Monica White

My work is so much a part of my life in the community and with my family that it is hard to see where one stops and another starts. I could never just settle for a quiet family life, just doing the washing and getting the tea or sitting in front of the telly. I think I would die. I have no idea what is going on at the moment on the TV, though I watch it sometimes to relax. My family is my top priority, and I like a good dance and a little party if I can. But I have to keep busy. So far I have found that my family can be incorporated into the things I do outside. If I'm looking after a baby I would not stay here doing nothing else. I would take it along with me. I have been in youth work since 1973, and *that* all came about through my own children really.

WORKING IN THE COMMUNITY

When my children were smaller we went to a Church of England church. I could see that the kids there ended up with nothing to do. They used to go over to the Vicarage, and the priest didn't have a clue on how to amuse them because he was a single man, a single priest, and we ended up thinking, "How

---

Monica White was born in Jamaica and since 1962 has lived in London. She works as a community organiser - currently running the Chestnuts Community & Arts Centre *in Harringey. She has four children - Lorenzo, Pat, Michael and Claire - and six grandchildren - Omari, Akilah, Chellon, Parys, Michaela and Dion.*

could we give them something to do?" So I would give them
tenpence each and they put it together and the priest would
buy some squash as they were always at his fridge. And they
used to play ping-pong on the table. Soon they started looking
forward to going up to the Vicarage, and that's where it all
began. We started organising things like trips out to the
theatre, and a disco at the church hall. The girls would clean
the hall and the boys would build speaker boxes and borrow
records from friends. Then in 1987 there was a fire in New
Cross, when a lot of black children died, maybe twelve or
thirteen children. We organised a dance to raise some money
for that. We raised money in this church hall and it was so
popular it became a regular thing.

The youth service was having a problem with a youth club
at the time. They must have heard about us, and asked if they
could use our hall. They had trained youth workers, and I
thought that if I've been doing the same thing all that time,
unofficially, I might as well get some training for it. The
whole thing escalated into me becoming a part-time youth and
community worker. Since then it has been cut back, and that
bit of the church building had to be sold to a Pentecostal
group. But through it I became established within the borough.
I have also done a lot of fundraising for all types of causes. I
used to belong to a women's group, and helped write a book
called *The Heart of the Race* with Stella Dadzie and others,[13]
and worked on things like the SUS campaign. I'm a paid up
member for the Jamaica environmental programme too. I get
involved with whatever goes on in the community. I can't stop.

I'm involved in a Youth club in Jamaica as well. We
formed this group to raise funds to see if we can help people
there. So far we have given money for a church in Kingston
and for some buildings for a children's ward. For many years
I was on the executive of the Cultural Centre, and that was a
long and taxing thing. For a while I was also chair of the
education thing. We got some money from the TEC, and I set
up an after-school and homework club. I used to pick up all

the children in about seven schools in Stamford Hill, Crouch End and so on. But I couldn't be at more than one place at the same time so I was often late. The teachers were very good about it. They would say, "Here comes Mrs. White," and used to be sitting down with the children and have them all ready. Then I would take them up to the West Indian Centre and settle them down. I had two people working for me and they never used to get on, and I used to sort them out and then I gave the children tea. And afterwards I would take them home. I did that for a year until the new Centre was underway.

All that nearly killed me because I used to be running back from there and picking up the grandchildren and coming back to the Chestnut Centre and people would be outside waiting for me before they could get in and I'd have to apologise. I just had to do it all because it needed to be done. The Centre has survived, even though I have had to go to court over the debts. People said that there was no way I could do it on my own, but I turned it around. It is a challenge that has worked. I can't see anything pass by - because that's my personality.

A TYPICAL DAY

My day usually begins when the telephone starts to ring at around seven in the morning. This morning I had been on the phone at 3.30 to my sister who called me from America for an hour. Then by seven this morning I was on the phone again to someone regarding an idea to do with a health programme. I need to give someone some papers to look at. Then there was another call coming in, and it was a woman making arrangements for Bernie's funeral.[14] These calls are usually to do with the Centre or a project to do with the Centre. That takes me to about eight, when I go to have a shower and a coffee.

This morning I also talked to a friend in Newcastle who needed cheering up. She always says, "I'm down, cheer me up." I make her laugh. After that I will come down and feed my cat, and put some clothes in the washing machine. I'm not the world's best housekeeper: but reasonable. So I try and do a bit of that. I'll just do the vacuuming today, and leave cleaning the other rooms until tomorrow. Ironing is something that I do when I can, and I may step in and do the ironing for a couple of hours for my children and grands.

I go over to the Centre at about nine, because I have to look after the security. There may be a wedding, or something for the pensioners, or a Turkish or Polish wedding, or African. So I show them around. I have to do the cleaning as well. I used to clean with the children there too. I had to do it virtually nonstop for five years to get the building meeting the health and safety standard and back functioning properly, to enable the local people to use it. I don't know how I fit all the hours into the day. Then I have to go to the bank or to a meeting. And I may get another call about going to the school.

The grandchildren are always with me as I am always being called to pick them up. So that's a typical day. I juggle. I pick up Omari and then I pick up Dion, then I take them back and give them chips and sausage. Or I have to have something in the car for them to eat when I go to the Centre.

The earliest that I can go to bed is about midnight on a good day. The Centre finishes as late as ten, and if there are any functions that go on until very late then I have to care-take after that. I leave there about eleven and come in and have a shower and get into bed and watch a bit of TV. Don't ask me how I do it. Friends do ask, and I just cannot settle down long enough to explain. If I look at a book I'll read two lines and fall asleep.

I'm not a very relaxed person. My telephone is always ringing. I care-take weekend functions, and try to fit in going to church on a Sunday. I even manage the Centre at the end of the phone from as far away as Portugal and Jamaica. I now have a lady who cleans three times a week. And that is a god-send. But there is always some sort of cleaning that has to be done, and I still have to clean at night if we have had a

wedding or conference or something. Somebody opens the first
security lock for me. But it used to be open up in the
mornings, come back here, then take the kids to school. One
used to go to school in Walthamstow, which is quite far. I
have to drop them off. Then I go to the shop to get some bits
and pieces before I go to the Centre.

When I arrive I get, "Monica where were you, we called
you three times, la la la?." And they expect me to make an
apology. But I can't do all of the things at the same time. We
have something different every day. There's Karate this
evening. So I'll finish by nine so I can go and see Bernie's
wake. Tomorrow I'll do some painting, and in the evening I've
got to go to a meeting somewhere to do with the Mayor. Then
I've got to go to Westminster to see someone. Is it Nyrere?
Something to do with that anyway. Then tonight I've got to go
over to the youth club and see if that's okay. I may finish by
ten. Some nights I do, some nights I don't. I just jumble
myself all around.

BRINGING THE CHILDREN ALONG

I am so busy it is ridiculous. But I do enjoy my work, and I
feel motivated. If there is a problem I always like to get
involved in sorting it out. And it does not stop me spending
time with my grandchildren. They are aged five to sixteen, and
although they do not live with me they are often with me. In
the day and overnight they are all with me sometimes. I may
pick them up or take them somewhere, or they just like to
hang around with me. That's nice. Some of them live in the
East End, but others are not too far away. The older ones come
over by themselves, and the younger ones get dropped off by
their parents and spend the weekend here. I used to take them
to school when they were much younger, but now I do the
picking up. Or it may be holiday time so they stay here.

Chellon does not come over often, because she's furthest
away. But I go over to her mother's house. We went to see a

play on Mother's Day. Her mother is into art and theatre work. She teaches at a school, and Chellon works behind the scenes. They put on a lot of black historical plays and all that. They have a performance company, and they invited me to the Mother's Day show this year.

The younger ones love coming to stay with me. They love being around me you know, because I'm always whizzing around and if they're with me they come along so we can have a chat in the car about what they have been up to, or anything that they can find to quiz me about when I was a child back home. If we're going places that's what I do. We've been on holiday, I've taken them with me on holiday before. We've been to America, and Jamaica, and in this country. Not all of them at once, just one or two at a time. I would have loved to take them all on holiday, though, and have a great big family reunion - well not reunion but get-together. It would cost a lot of money though, so that's got to be just a dream. Maybe they could pay for themselves one day. But it's just getting them all to get time off at the same time. The children are all so busy. Everybody seems to be busy doing their own thing.

I remember the first time I took my four children away. I took them to America, and my older son was just about sixteen and it was his first plane ride and he turned to me when we took off at Heathrow and said, "Thank you mum." We went to stay at my ex-husband's sister's place in Manhattan, and we went on that cruise around the place. I've been to America and Jamaica with Chellon and her Dad and Michael and then Akilah and then Dion - but not Omari. So he's the only one who hasn't had a holiday with me on his own.

I like to take them out when I can. Whenever I had a bit of free time what I used to do was get a picnic together and stuff like that, or we would go to the theatre or to a restaurant. Or maybe have a nice little dinner party here at home. We invite people to come over, and in summer we have barbecues, depending on the weather. We used to have so many barbecues here. But during the last few years, since the Centre has taken up most of my time, and because I haven't been very well, I haven't been able to organise one. What I did - not this year but the year before - was have a very lovely Christmas dinner with all the children and all the grandchildren.

I wanted to go away to be honest, but I thought "I can't afford it." When I had to get the Christmas presents I thought I can't afford that either, with all the family getting larger and larger and with all these adverts on television all these Nintendo and everything. So I thought what can I do to let us be a family? I've got a friend who's like 'cordon bleu', and we said it will be a nice idea to have a dinner party. So I had 'Kwanzaa' - which is a black celebration like a Thanksgiving. A friend of mine came over and printed the list on his computer. We had soup 'a la carte', and sweet potato pie, pork and roast duck and a turkey and beef and all different meats, roast potatoes and parsnips and salad and gateaux, and it was nice with champagne on the table and we had these nice little name plates with everybody's name on it and everybody was together.

I did it at the Centre because I had the space there. I just had to think of what I could do for everybody together. In the end I had thirty-two people. The men played dominoes after the meal, the children played games, and we danced. They all enjoyed it, and keep asking me to put it on again. But I said not this year. I would have loved it, but I've been too busy because the Centre has been so busy.

I get involved with the children at school too. Recently there was some sort of special event for International Women's Day. They put on a play at the school, and I had to stop and attend it, and when I got there I became involved in organising it. I was in the kitchen a lot of the time because I can't stop it. If I see something done in a way that I don't think is going to look good I start saying, "Do this," and "Do that." I stayed on the door for a bit to collect money too. I also used to be a school governor. I was the chair of governors for a year but that was very taxing because of all the meetings. I also go to church and sometimes take the children. I'm on the PCC there, and I was a church warden at some stage.

I think that the children will see that I'm active, and from that they will learn something. I love to encourage them with their lessons and education. I'd like to see them travel and experiencing things. I love travelling. I'm trying to encourage Akilah and Chellon to do some travelling. I see Akilah more and encourage her to learn Spanish and French. If they need me they can just call me and I shall be there.

A BREAK WITH TRADITION

All of this is very different to the life I would have led if I had stayed in Jamaica. At home we would have seen my parents, aunts, cousins, and all the family together. The grandchildren would have liked to see their grandfather as well, so we would all be together in a community. Their grandfather lives in South London now. He does not see much of them. He never was much of a family person - though I think maybe he regrets that now.

We do have lots of cousins here but they are all scattered. I would like to bring them all a bit closer. I try to see if I can hold the family together as much as I can. Me and my children have got a good rapport, so we can talk about anything. And also the grandchildren. They see me as grandmother and grandfather combined - as the person trying to be both these people. As the person keeping it all together.

In Jamaica it was tradition to keep the family all together at home in the same place. Grandma would be on the veranda you know. We wouldn't have old people's homes; it was the family's responsibility to look after them. When I first came here I couldn't believe that grandparents didn't live at home with the children. It was like a foreign language to me. I felt that she's supposed to be here - that it was the family responsibility. Now the same thing that happened to white people is happening to the black people who have come here.

My mother was never really a grandmother with us as she was in Jamaica and my children were all born here. She did not come here until she was eighty. I wanted her to be near the children - it was something I used to often dream about - and I could not afford for them all to be near her there. So she lived here. I brought her over, and she spent a year with me; but she was going blind. I had to look after her, and I had to go to work at the same time. But she was able to see the grandchildren, which was good.

So being here has broken a lot of tradition for me. As I get older I don't find myself getting like my mother. Although I'm getting older I've got a young heart and mind. My mother was very quiet. I've always got to be involved in something. I've been a bit of a tomboy and I've always got to say something. In my young days I would see something I didn't like and my Mum would say to me, "You mustn't say anything," and I would say back, "No, I can't help it." My Mum was very timid: I was a bit of a challenger.

I had to do it for my children, too. In the early years I had to be at home for them. But after I was divorced I realised that I had to go to work and look after my children and take them to school. I brought the children up on my own, and it was very hard really, very hard. We went through some rough times, but thank God I'm through it. It was very, very trying. I had to find a decent enough job to be able to put some food on the table. It hasn't been easy at all. And I thought that it wasn't enough, and that I wanted to become a bit more involved. So I joined the women's group, and then joined the school governors, and then went into a bit of local politics, and ran for councillor.

That is how it started. One thing I have not done though is study. I would love to do that. I have done many short training courses, but it would be an experience to study something in depth for a degree. However, for the moment I am far too busy.

A CONTINUOUS REVOLUTION

Jean Marjot

There are not any particular periods when things have changed more than others in my family. Change has taken place all of the time, and if I compare the lives of succeeding generations they are really quite different from each other, though not moving in any simple or single direction.

My maternal grandmother lived with my parents for the whole of my childhood. She was old and frail, and I don't think of her as a very involved granny. But I suppose that she must have been, as she was part of the daily life of the family. Although profoundly deaf - and she had a marvellous ear-trumpet that I wish I had kept - she read to me endlessly and taught me to read at an early age. She did a lot of the cooking, and I am sure that she helped my mother when I, and then later my brother, were babies. She was always there if my parents went out in the evening, so they did not have to worry about finding a baby-sitter.

In many ways my grandmother must have been quite lonely though. She had lost both her sons in the first world war, and her husband had died not long afterwards. So she was always rather living in the past. We lived in huge Methodist Manses, in South Wales, Westmorland, Lancashire and Cumbria, and

Jean Marjot lives in Surrey with her husband David who is a retired consultant psychiatrist, formerly a naval doctor. Before having children she worked as a nurse. They now have four sons and a daughter, plus twelve grandchildren ranging in age from four to fifteen.

she always had a big bedroom, where I can remember taking her supper up to her on a tray. She read there interminably, and kept mainly to herself. I can recall her reading *Gone with the Wind*. I suppose I was about twelve at the time, and I asked her if I could read it too, and she said, "No dear! Oh, no dear! It's not very nice." But of course I read it anyway. I can remember later on my father would not let me go to see *Pygmalion*, because it had the word bloody in it. What a different world it was to today's.

I can just about remember when my brother was born, when I was four. As soon as my mother started to go into labour I had to go and sleep in Grandma's bed. She had a great big double bed. In those days they used to have maternity nurses who moved in to take charge of things during the birth and stay for a week or two afterwards. I didn't really hear a thing. Next morning Grandma said, "You've got a baby brother," and I suppose I was vaguely interested. I was given a new china doll and a little pram to push.

We were sent to boarding school when we were quite young, and often stayed with relatives in the holidays because it was wartime and our house had been bombed. So as we got older and grew up we did not see that much of her, and left her behind with our childhood.

LIFE IN THE NAVY

The childhood of my own offspring was not at all like this, because my husband David was in the Navy and during the early years we were often away on foreign postings. One son was born abroad in Singapore, and it was not possible for our relatives to help. Instead of grannies, we had Amahs.

This was in the good old days when people who could afford it had servants - a 'baby Amah' to nurse the children, a cook, a driver - called a Syce - and a Kabûn who was the gardener. Although I did lot of the cooking, we did have an Amah who also did all of the washing, ironing and babysitting.

Everyone in the military quarters in Singapore had them,
and we just found the staff we needed by word of mouth
really. People just passed them on. The first time that we were
out there we had rented quarters on an estate with enormous
numbers of Army and Air Force people there too. The second
time we got an army quarter, because David was working at
the British military hospital. We were the only naval family on
the patch. But it was very pleasant, with lovely houses, and the
children went to the Army school.

I didn't go out to work. Quite a lot of mothers did go to
work in Singapore. But I didn't so I looked after the children,
and took them swimming all afternoon. School was from 8.00
a.m. to 1.00 p.m. We had the rest of the day to ourselves, and
could take the homework to do at the pool. In the evening I
would put them to bed. The Amah cooked some of the meals,
and then used to get up early and clean the house. A lot of
people there I know went off and left their children full-time
with the Amahs, which I would not have wanted to do. Some
parents actually went to Hong Kong on holiday and left their
children with the Amahs for the whole time.

AMAHS IN PLACE OF GRANNIES

David's mother and father had been against us getting married,
and it was quite some time before they - particularly David's
father - got round to being proper grandparents to our children.

My mother was there when my second son was born - when
we were in married quarters in Littlehampton. She came down,
supposedly to help, but was such a nuisance that I was glad
when she went away. I am sure that she was very fond of the
children. She came to see us off at Heathrow afterwards, when
we went back to Singapore. In those days you could walk right
up to the aeroplane. Heathrow was just a few huts. She came
up to the plane and was quite sorry to see us go, and wrote
straight away. David's mother wrote more regularly, by then,
and sent quite a lot of presents out, and of course we

reciprocated. But when we got back from Singapore neither of them seemed overjoyed to see us.

But I was sorry that none of them came out at all. The airlines used to have 'Granny Flights' - which were cheap flights out for grandparents at certain times of the year. Quite a lot of people had their parents come out to visit them. There were times when I thought it would be lovely to show them around, and to do this or that with them.

They would not have been able to do much in the way of helping with the children if they had come though. It was too hot. The temperature was about a 100⁰F degrees for most of the time. On the rare occasions when I was without an Amah for a few days, while a new one was coming, I would stand naked to do the ironing - simply dripping with sweat and with an overhead fan on. It was so, so hot. In Singapore the temperature doesn't vary very much. In Hong Kong there are seasons. But in Singapore it was hot and sweaty all the year round. You got used to it. But nowadays of course everywhere is air-conditioned: so you don't get used to it.

But our Amahs were as useful as grandparents - particularly the one we had when our third son Christopher was born. We had a Malay Amah called Jelimah. Most people had Chinese Amahs, but I liked the Malays because they were much kinder and more easy-going. She was with the children all the time from before Christopher was born, until we finally came home - when she was brought to the airport to say goodbye to us and we were all in tears.

I remember when Jelimah came to the hospital to pick me up with Christopher. You couldn't have a baby at home in Singapore, and I wouldn't go to the military hospital, so I was taken to the Chinese hospital and discharged myself the next day. Jelimah came to collect me and I said to her, "Another boy, Jelimah," and she said, "That's all right, Mem." And she was marvellous. I would leave Christopher asleep in his pram and go to the shops with the other two and when I came back she was always standing on the verandah with him in her arms

- just as a grandma would have done. She was in fact a grandmother herself - which was lovely. I can remember saying to David just before we left, "She's been more like a mother to me than my own mother during these years." The Amahs we had had before were younger, and a bit like au pairs now. They wanted to go off after about six months to do something else.

When we visited Singapore a few years later I was determined to go and see Jelimah, and I'd kept the address of the kampong where she lived. I think these kampongs don't exist any more. Everything is just a mass of concrete flats. Anyway, we got into a taxi and gave the driver the address. He said, "Oh, you can't go there, Mem, you can't go there." But I said, "Yes I can." And she was just overjoyed to see us. But in the interval of just a few years she had grown older than she would have done had it been in UK. Also she was diabetic and going blind. But she threw her arms around Christopher and cuddled and kissed him, in a lot of consternation. That's just like a grandma.

MY OWN TURN AS GRANDMOTHER

With my own grandchildren the position is different again. I am not part of their daily life like my grandmother was of mine. But David and I live reasonably near to all of them most of the time. We can see them often and be there to help out if we are needed. This is very important to me, and in fact my whole life changed when my first grandchild was born. I was fifty-eight years old, and recovering from breast cancer, when Chris lifted the baby out of the crib just a few hours after his birth and said, "You have waited a long time for this moment." I held this tiny baby boy in my arms and realised that this new life indeed meant the beginning of a new life for me too.

A great joy! And being a grandmother is quite different from being a parent. For one thing you are more conscious of danger to them, and while admiring the things that grandchildren do we also worry more about them at the same time. When any of them come to stay I am up many times in the night to take a look and see if they are OK. I sleep so much more lightly then. I do know that other grandparents move into the same bedroom, or take the little one into their own bed with them, in order to know that they are safe and sound all night. I rather think this is a common practice.

Modern grandparents are on the whole probably able to do more than earlier generations to entertain their grandchildren. We have enjoyed many a pantomime, circus, theatre and cinema in a way that our own grandparents were not able to do. And of course with cars travel has become easier and more common. We are always dropping in to see them, or having some of them to stay with us.

For instance, when Christopher and Eleni's children took it in turns to have chickenpox, we had first of all one to convalesce with us and then the others. That way they could be looked after a bit more. And we loved having them: as when Robert and Carol popped over to France and left the three of theirs with us. This is something that neither of my children's grandparents would ever have done – though I do realise that in some circumstances many grandparents of that generation did have a great deal of responsibility for the children.

We visited Robert and Carol in Australia a few years ago when they were living there, and stayed on a tropical island with them. Their first son was about eighteen months old at the time, and took charge of us completely. Early in the morning, while his mother slept, we would walk along the tropical beach, picking up shells and waiting to see the sunrise. A truly magical time. I have always felt sorry that I was not out there when their second was born.

Huw, Felicity's oldest boy, comes and sleeps with us quite often. They only live in Weybridge so that's not very far away. He is fond of ringing me up early in the morning. "Good morning, Grandma," he will say, followed by any news such as, "I have got chickenpox," and asking when he can see us. He likes to spend the night with us, and we love to have him. He likes the old books such as Tintin and Asterix, which I have kept from my own children and which I put by his bed.

I think that if our daughter-in-law Lizzie had been alive we would have had the girls to stay probably on their own by now. But since her tragic death Tim does not really like to part with them. She died of cancer a couple of years ago. He is pleased if we're there, to help look after them if he has gone abroad or something. He knows that he can always call us and we'll go straight down there.

That was a hard thing to deal with. When Lizzie was ill in hospital having chemotherapy we used to visit them a lot. At that time they had a very good German au pair, who was superb really. The youngest was only three months old, so she had to be a mother really to that child. Lizzie's mother had died when she was about fifteen I think. Lizzie did not have much contact with her father and step-mother. They did not live nearby. So for a while we did have them to stay a lot. The au pair used to come along too, and she was a really great girl and was very, very good with the children and in fact she still keeps in touch with them after all this time.

The girls were two and four when their mother died, two years ago now. They have been surprisingly adaptable. Lizzie was too ill to look after them for a long time. The girls at that time had a very good French au pair, Sandrine, who still keeps in touch with us.

She stayed longer than originally intended. She came for three months then Tim asked her to stay longer. She has been to see them recently. She was a great help, and I did admire her because she was only very young.

John and Linda's two boys, Oliver and Alistair, live in Guildford and do come and stay with us quite often. They are still quite young, but also are delightful company. John is our eldest son, and obviously has an important position in the family.

So we always seem to be busy. I adored having children, and I loved being a mother. And I suppose I adore being a grandmother too. But I can't do as much for them as I was doing for my own children. I am very happy to be involved if they need me. The family are growing up now – the oldest ones are fifteen, thirteen and twelve – so they have lots of things of their own to do. But they still come over. They've been several times recently. I find that the nicest time is when they're all here together. That is quite hectic these days. They all go out into the garden and play rugby. And the uncles and the fathers go out too, and it's an absolute scream to watch them. The bigger boys are getting stronger and rougher than the uncles. It's hilarious. Then everybody comes in and feeds. To me that is the essence of being a grandmother.

EXPERIENCED HANDS

FINDING OUT WHAT IS IMPORTANT

Jane Taylor

My life as a grandmother has been very much influenced by
the fact that two of my daughters live in America, so that
keeping in touch takes some organisation. There are some
drawbacks to them being there, but also plenty of benefits and
compensations. I think also that it helps me to see more clearly
which things are most important in life.

A LONG-DISTANCE GRANNY

I had a sort of sixth sense when Catherine became pregnant.
We had not spoken for a while, and when she rang I somehow
knew what she was going to say. It made me feel very mixed.
I was happy for her. But I was also sad that they were so far
away, and I would not be able to spend much time with her.
I had a child at school, James, who was still quite young, so
I knew I was of course tied here. Catherine probably felt the
same, but this did not show up until I went over for the birth.

One of the things you realise when you're apart, when
you're in different countries, is that you want to have quality
time together. Whenever she visited we would make sure to
take her out on her own, and spend time with her. It was still

---

*Jane Taylor is a retired nurse living in North London with her husband
Maurice. She has three daughters, two of whom live in Chicago, and
one son. There are four grandchildren - three in the US through her
oldest daughter Catherine and one in London through her middle
daughter Rachel.*

a shock to think that she might stay in America. She had known Jeff for about three years there before getting married. Even after the marriage I still kidded myself that he would find a job over here in a few years and they would be back. A child made it less likely.

Catherine came over to London before Jacob was born, and we had a very happy time. She was feeling well, and there were lots of things to do. I entered into the spirit of it by making a lot of clothes for him, and clothes for his cot and things like that. Then I gave her as long as I could in America when he was born. I went over a week or two before he was due, and stayed on for a month or so afterwards. And it was only when I was leaving that it really hit home to me - to both of us I think - how vulnerable she was to be with a first child and not in her own country. That was quite hard.

Also Catherine had her own life there. She had been working in a charity organisation, but was at university when Jacob was born. I can remember taking Jacob up to the university when he was a few days old for her to breastfeed during her breaks. Maurice had found someone to look after James and had come over himself after the birth. We drove Jacob to the university together, and Catherine would come out to the car and feed him.

Over the years, as more grandchildren have arrived, we have got used to the idea that they are going to remain there, and to see benefits in it as well. It has been very interesting going off to America regularly, and having grandchildren who are brought up in a slightly different way. In many respects we've thoroughly enjoyed it, and have gone from a rather negative attitude at first to a much more positive one now.

For one thing, we have had some nice surprises in the schools there. Jacob, who is now twelve, plays the violin. He has joined the school orchestra very quickly and we have noticed that the way they treat them in the orchestra is very professional. They do concerts and dress up for them in bow ties, and this really seems to stimulate them.

They have some very enterprising teaching methods in subjects like history too. For example Tessa, who is now nine, had to dress up and spend the day as a 'pioneer mother' a few weeks ago. Catherine made her costume - a bonnet and long dress. Tessa had an older boy as her husband, plus five children who were children from younger classes and a baby (a doll) of course. They had to do things like de-hydrate their food, because this is what the pioneers did, and had a wagon which they had to drag along the street for about half a mile and take into the nearest woods - which happened to be called Thatcher Woods, which was quite amusing for me.

They spent the day in the woods, with Indians coming upon them (that was parents dressed up, and some older children) and bartering food for jewellery with them. They dragged their wagon through the muddy wood and came across some other Indians, and did a dance in pioneer style, and so on. Then they dragged it all the way back again. The marvellous costumes that the mums had made got rather muddy. The children went off looking absolutely beautiful and came back thoroughly bedraggled - but very happy. That sort of thing is very different from an English school.

HOLDING THE FAMILY TOGETHER

We see our 'American family' three times a year at the moment. We go over there for two weeks in early Spring. They come over to stay with us for a month in the summer. And then we go over again in the autumn, in late October. So we see the grandchildren every three or four months, which is lovely.

Inevitably it is easier to stay close to grandchildren if you see them often. My middle daughter Rachel has a son, Giacomo, who is ten now and lives only a few minutes away from us. There has been a continuity with him right from the start. Rachel has always worked, and I've had him right from a very young age, once a week or more, except when we're away. Rachel is divorced now, but Giacomo sees his dad every week. His other grandmother is in Italy - his grandfather has died - and he is going to stay there with her for part of the summer. Otherwise he is often round here.

I do find that I have a very good rapport with Giacomo. We have some lovely chats together, about simple things. We have got a lot of memories, and can say when we're out somewhere, "Do you remember when this happened, do you remember that?" For years one of the things we've been doing is tea after school. Maurice will fetch him from school, once or twice a week, and when they get back in the car I will always have ready a simple tea, all laid out. As they get here I make him cheese-on-toast. And then the idea is that neither of us can get up from the table. The tea is made, and pot full, and neither of us can get up from the table. If we do, we lose points. And if Maurice joins us, he does too. It's a stupid thing, but it does mean that you can talk. In a kitchen it is so easy to be up and down all the time at meals. We have done that sort of thing for years - so I am bound to feel close to him.

I was not particularly close to my own mother. I loved her, but we never did things together. I loved my granny too, but she had very severe arthritis so she was always an invalid, and could not pick us up for example. It was during the war and we didn't see them very often anyway. So I don't think that I got much idea from either of them how to be a grandmother. A lot of what I do comes from my own feelings about the things I would have liked to have done with my own children but did not have the time for. A quiet tea with a nice chat. It seemed just a dream when I had four children to look after - plus extra people quite often. But with Giacomo I can achieve it.

It is partly that there is only one of him. But mainly it is how often I see him. When I go to America it is usually the term time, and I'll walk Tessa to school and we'll sing all the old songs from *The King and I*, and I'll teach her the old musicals. These are the sorts of things I do with her, and I feel a rapport with her. But it is not quite the same as with Giacomo, where the nearness makes it so much easier, and where I am able to see him a lot without being busy. There's a much freer spirit within me when I am not bogged down with housework etc.

A while ago I started to feel that I was not quite so close to Jacob, and I have made a concerted effort over the last few visits to improve this. It has paid off enormously. For example, he plays the violin and Catherine, who has a new, part-time law course, can't be with them all the time. So I sit with him while he practices, and encourage him. Everyday things like that help a lot. And when I leave for England I say to him, "Come on, give me a kiss." And if he doesn't want to I'll chase him round the kitchen table and he gives me a hug in the end. So we have a lot of fun together, and our relationship has improved by leaps and bounds.

Henry, their youngest, is easy because he is still very little really. You just have to play bricks with him, and do shunting noises when he is pushing trains; things like that. And take him to the park. But as they get older it is a bit more subtle.

Every year we *all* meet up. It is very important. The American family all stay in the house, and Giacomo comes to stay too. Our son James who lives near will come in a lot and Alison, our other daughter, who also lives in Chicago, will be here with her boy-friend too. We don't have enough room to put them all up and so we have to spread them out among friends in the terrace.

It is quite a crowd. The main worry for me, as the one in charge, is making sure that they are looked after - the shopping and the cooking and making sure that there are enough toilet rolls in the house. Basic stuff. When we go there we get looked after, and I try to make sure that it is the same for them when they come here.

It is so good to see all the grandchildren together. The Americans love Giacomo, and he loves them, and they fall into him as easily as anything. The boys are all keen on sport, and link up with neighbours too for tennis and football. They do it every year. If there was a bigger gap, I think that it would be more difficult for them.

I think that being a grandmother has made me very grateful for my family. They do seem to want to see each other, and to enjoy each other's company. It is always the same old familiar house here for them. The children all have the same bedrooms every time. It is very gratifying for me that they want to come back here each year.

THE FAMILY THAT PRAYS TOGETHER

Being a grandmother has definitely made me think more about families - particularly as part of my family is separated. I think that I have always felt that good family life is the key to the health of the nation. I feel it as strongly as that. This has become emphasised more and more as I have grown older, and especially as I have become a grandmother. Therefore it has made me feel very thankful; but also very aware that Maurice and I both have a very important part to play in this spread-out family. It may seem a bit idealistic, but I feel that unselfishness and those sorts of qualities are absolutely key, and you must help to develop them as far as you can.

Being a Christian makes a very big difference as well. The general attitude of current society toward families is not all very helpful. One of the really sad things, which I really feel in my heart, is that mothers often don't feel free to stay at home any more. There is a great big push in the collective psyche to get mothers out to work as quickly as possible. It is to do with the materialistic age we live in. People want a lot more. We all do. But to me the really sad thing is that if somebody says to you at a party, "What do you do?" and you answer, "Oh, I don't do anything," what it means is, "I am just a housewife."

That says it all. And I don't think that people - that is young mothers - feel that they have a real choice. If you have

got money worries, then you may have to work. And some
people positively prefer to hand over their child to somebody
else when they're young. But they should not be pushed.

I was a nurse before I had children, and I stopped working
when they were young. This meant that there was more time
for them - though I never felt that I was brilliant with them,
especially when they were really young. I would have liked a
two-day-a-week job for some of the period. I did go back part-
time to nursing when all my four children were at school. But
I wasn't retrained, and found the new treatments and
procedures very difficult, so I only stuck it for a couple of
years. I did some other jobs after that, but I think that I would
have been happier if I had managed to keep my hand in at
nursing. But the time that you have at different stages of your
children's life changes, and you need flexibility to fit in with
that. They must come first. Family life, especially for the
mother who is the centre of the home, is constant adjustment.
And that is why choice is important.

Another thing which has happened in modern living is the
disappearance of eating together. When our family comes
together every summer, the most important times are when we
can sit and eat together and talk - the evening meal in
particular, though we don't always manage it. We all have
turns in preparing the food, and I think this is very important.
The shared meal is a very practical way of keeping in touch.
Jews have this very strongly in their religion, with the family
meal on Friday. It is a very big thing for them.

Religion means a lot to all of our family; all our children
are on a journey of faith. We all find as a family that praying
for each other is important. If Catherine is feeling that one of
the children is a bit low or sick she'll phone and say to me,
"Would you pray." And they'll do the same for us. So they all
have a faith of some sort.

The family that prays together, stays together.

THE STEP-GRANDMOTHER'S EXPERIENCE

Kate Gavron

I am in a different position to all the other contributors to this volume. Some may also be step-mothers, even step-grandmothers, but they are all mothers (if not yet grandmothers). I will almost certainly never be a mother and I will therefore never be a 'real' grandmother. My husband has two sons from one marriage and two daughters from another and he has five grandchildren, with another one due in the summer of 2000. I am therefore a step-grandmother and it is a relationship which gives me enormous pleasure. My step-children might be surprised to know that I consider their children to be of central importance in my life.

I believe that my feeling of closeness to them is largely because I have known all these grandchildren since they were born; they all live in London, as I do, and I have seen them regularly throughout their lives. This is a difference between my step-children and step-grandchildren and I believe it is one of the most critical factors in building up a close relationship with growing children, whatever the nature of the tie with them.

I have no regrets that I do not have children myself. Apart from any other reasons, I know that more children would

Kate Gavron worked in publishing for fifteen years before training as a social anthropologist and researcher. She is currently engaged in a number of research projects at the Institute of Community Studies, *and is Deputy Chair of the* Runnymede Trust's *Commission on the Future of Multi-Ethnic Britain.*

almost certainly have caused stresses and strains in all the extended family relationships, particularly between my step-children and myself, and between them and their father. However, steps are the only children and grandchildren that I will have, and I am dependent on them to be part of my future family and family life.

Although I have no regrets for myself I have one regret which causes me grief: I have not given my own parents any grandchildren. They are devoted and good grandparents to their two grandsons, my sister's children, but from their three children they deserve more than these two grandsons to display in the competitive world of grandparenthood. My parents know my step-children and grandchildren but their relationship is just too distant and the time they entered each others' lives is just too late for these to replace any grandchildren they could have known from birth as my own children.

The question for which I have to wait to discover the answer is what happens after my husband dies before me (statistically extremely probable, due to our ages). Will all the years of contact, especially with my step-grandchildren ever since their births, be enough to earn me a permanent place in their extended family, or will they disappear from my life? This is a question which 'real' grandparents rarely have to ask themselves.

It is undoubtedly the case that paternal grandparents can and do effectively lose their grandchildren after an acrimonious divorce, but this is relatively rare. This for me is one of the most telling differences between the 'true' grandchild and the step-grandchild. Because relationships with young children are mediated through their parents it is my step-children who will give or deny access to their children, until the children are older.

My grandchildren have a lot of grandparents: three grandsons have a grandmother and grandfather in the USA and two step-grandmothers and a grandfather living near them in London. My two grand-daughters have all their five grandparents (including the two step-grannies) in London. The baby due in a few weeks time will have four grandparents and three step-grandparents, all living nearby. How overwhelming this sounds for such a small baby. And yet, and yet, how many of this great quantity of grandparents will be around to give much help? I suspect not many, certainly not the kind of help that could make much difference to the lives of two working parents.

All seven grandparents have lives full of work, travel, friends, other children, other grandchildren. I do not envisage any of the fellow grandparents of this baby slowing down their lives very often to the slow beat of a toddler's routine. The whole family suffers from hurry-sickness and excess of choice and opportunity and we are not alone.

MY OWN GRANDPARENTS

When I look back at my own childhood, like most others I remember infinite time. Two of my own grandparents were very important in my life, two died when I was very young. I have a shadowy memory of looking down through the railings into the basement of my paternal grandparents' house and seeing my grandmother there. I think she was on the floor making clothes for us but this may be my invention. I have a vague impression of my mother's father as a quiet, calm presence, but my memory may be no more than the impression gained from family photographs: a grave, handsome man with a moustache and pipe.

I understand that he was certainly not regarded as a 'calm' presence by many other people, least of all by his legal colleagues, but there is a photographic record of him playing with his grandson, my brother, as a baby, and this confirms my early impression. Like many grandfathers of his generation, I expect he was spared the worst excesses of his grandchildren's behaviour and we were probably removed from his company when things got difficult.

My father's father also had a moustache and pipe but I remember them clearly and loved him dearly. He lived near us, we saw him at least weekly and he spent many (probably frustrating) hours of my childhood patiently teaching me about musical harmony, counterpoint and composition. Because I was the middle child I was lucky in being chosen to go on special holidays alone with him, to stay with one of his sisters-in-law, my great-aunt. He would take me down in the train and look after me with my great-aunt's help and with no other child's company but I was totally happy in the company of these two delightful elderly relations in an ancient thatched cottage. I not only had the treat of holidays alone with my grandfather but also with my mother's mother, and I relished the undivided attention of two exceptional grandparents.

My mother's mother died when I was fifteen and I still miss her wonderfully benign and comforting presence. We spent every Sunday of my childhood with her and usually saw her on other occasions during the week; she joined us on many of the family holidays of my childhood; my siblings and I would stay with her on our own without our parents and, as a special treat, sometimes on our own without our siblings. She taught us how to play Bezique and poker; for breakfast she gave us – glory of glories – toast with the crusts cut off, and once in a while she even let us have a puff of her single daily Du Maurier cigarette. She seemed the perfect Granny: always with time for us, always on our side, sharing any successes and uncritical of failure. She provided typical middle-class Granny luxuries, such as my first red velvet party dress. I realise now that she did not in fact have as much energy as my child's eyes saw; she was in ill-health for a number of years before she died and my mother and aunts cared for her very much more than she cared for us. How those endless games of Bezique must have wearied her. But I was a child and I did not notice that, or the fact that she did not baby-sit for us when my parents went out. For me she was perfection because she always had time for me.

THE NEXT GENERATIONS

I do not play such a role in my grandchildren's lives, and I feel I should. I even *could*, if I organised my life to do so. But they are step-grandchildren and this makes things different. When I examine what happens in every-day life I realise that to some small extent I am wary of giving a hostage to fortune in the form of building close relationships of which I am not in control.

After nearly twenty years with their father I love all my step-children. However, when I think about the relationships I recognise that I feel closer to my step-daughters and realise that this is because of time. I have known them since they were younger and more dependent and, more importantly, I have known them for a greater part of *their* lives. We have more of their lives in common and more memories to share. I never remotely 'mothered' any of my step-children; my step-sons were almost adults when I started living with their father and my step-daughters were young teenagers. Their own mother, a wonderful woman, lived close to us and the girls never needed me as a mother in any sense. They did need their father, however, and they needed him on his own more than they needed us together; something I perhaps saw more easily than he did.

So even though I never mothered them in any way, I've been in their life since they were young and we share more of the history of their lives than I do their brothers'. We have also shared more holidays, weekends, evenings, put simply: time. I therefore have something more like a mother's experience with them as they have grown up, learned things, travelled and fallen in love. The girls' mother entered their brothers' lives when they were still young children and she shared their lives and truly mothered them as they grew up. The boys' mother had died and my husband's second wife was mother to the whole family, although the boys also had loving and attentive maternal grandparents of whom they saw a great deal.

The years have gone by and I adore and admire my step-children. It is an unheralded bonus of being a step-mother that I am able to talk about my step-daughters' beauty, charm and success to our friends without being boastful about my own offspring. As my elder step-daughter waits to have her first baby, I find myself wondering whether this baby will seem different to me, any more of a 'real' grandchild than his or her half-cousins because the baby's own mother is marginally more like a 'real' child to me. I don't believe this will happen because I believe that to a great extent the relationship with grandchildren depends largely on the grandparent and what he or she makes of it. With the exception of parents, other adults create their own relationships with new babies and small children; by spending time with them and becoming familiar faces with familiar voices.

Relationships with step-children (and step-parents) are notoriously vexed and difficult but they also vary enormously depending not only on individual behaviour and personality but also on when they started and in what circumstances. As far as grandchildren are concerned, babies mainly respond to the people who respond to them and familiarity seems to breed content: babies have to become children before they begin to understand the complexities of kinship diagrams and by then adults are, or are not, part of their lives. This is what I have in my relationship with my step-grandchildren, unlike my step-children: I was a fixed part of their world before they knew who I was.

I have been part of the flotsam and jetsam of my grandchildren's lives since they were born. As they grow up they are learning about the complexities of the typically chaotic twenty-first century families into which they have been born and how we all fit together. I hope they think of me as a permanent feature in their lives and they certainly seem to enjoy being with us, although like all grandparents we notice the approach of teenage taking the older children to new activities, more parties, more friends. We see them all regularly, however, and often all together, at some of the huge and noisy family parties we have, usually to celebrate one or more birthday, where everybody does meet, play and eat together. We also have children and grandchildren to stay in our holiday house, which gives us a good opportunity to spend unhurried time with them; especially important with the smaller children.

I do not have the experience of having my own children's children, but I know that no grandparent can take for granted the affection of their grandchildren without working for it. And like all grandparents I find any small arms outstretched in greeting totally beguiling and moving. I also know that the smallest arms do not stretch out because of blood ties but because of the strength of affection. I hope my presence now and in the future, when I hope the older grandchildren will be able to spend more time with us without their parents, will give me the kind of links with them that will not be broken by time and by new families, new hurries.

My grandchildren's parents are sensitive to this. One of the very happy moments of my adult life was when we returned from abroad to see a new baby, the eldest grand-daughter. As we admired her in the hospital where she had been born the day before, her father said to me that he and his partner wanted me to be as much a grandmother to her as all her other 'real' grandparents. I was moved because these gestures are important in step-relationships: unlike with one's own children, nothing can be taken for granted. New situations, like the arrival of the next generation, have to be tip-toed around gingerly as everybody adjusts to a new layer in the creaking edifice of the modern family.

WHERE WERE *YOU* IN THE REVOLUTION, GRANNY?

Patricia Neate

WATCHING FROM THE SIDELINES

The eye of the hurricane is a peaceful spot. It is only when it has passed over that the full effect of the storm is felt.

I met my husband at University when he was nineteen and I was twenty. We married three years later, in 1962, just as the storm clouds were gathering on the horizon. The Pill was shortly to come on the market, so we, incidentally, missed the sexual revolution by a whisker. We read the newly unexpurgated version of *Lady Chatterley's Lover* together with amusement and interest and John Thomas and Lady Jane entered our vocabulary along with other less romantic terms.

We then spent a period of study and work in the USA, while the Beatles were rising like rockets in the UK. We were quizzed there about the Profumo affair, although the main topics of social concern in the USA at that time were Civil Rights and the first stirrings of the Peace Movement. I had already been on a CND March in the UK. Women had an important voice in these movements, but feminism itself was not a big issue.

We returned to England to find the sixties in full swing and

Patricia Neate is a family therapist working in London. She has four grown-up children born in the late sixties and early seventies, two of whom are parents. Her first grandchild, born when she was fifty, is nearly ten. She has another grandson of five and a grand-daughter of eighteen months.

we started a family, so not a lot of swinging for us. The child-rearing guru of my generation was Dr. Benjamin Spock, whose reassuring approach chimed well with 'All You Need Is Love' and the Peace Movement in which he was to become a famous activist. By the time my second child was born in 1968 I was clear that I did not want to return to language teaching. Having attended some external university Sociology courses I embarked on counselling training, to be followed by Marriage Counselling and then, much later, Family Therapy. The effect of this was that as my family grew I was thinking seriously about the dynamics of couples and families and the needs of the individuals involved.

These ideas, starting with John Bowlby's theories around attachment and maternal deprivation, plus my own immersion in the day-to-day concerns of a young family, provided an interesting counterpoint to burgeoning radicalism. Looking back, I feel I became more an observer of than a participant in the gathering revolution, working increasingly with debates about values and social goals and the impact of these, both positive and negative, on the lives of clients across generations, as well as on the lives of my own family and friends. The answer to the question in my title is that I was pretty much on the sidelines. Sometimes cheering, sometimes booing, often confused.

Since those days I have talked with very many families as they work to find their way through difficult transitions and life crises. These conversations always take account of at least three generations with their different beliefs and aspirations, as well as the social and cultural context of their lives. Turning this lens on my own family is familiar. I suspect that most women analyse their families constantly. However, focusing on the role of grandmother has been new: thinking of myself as grandchild, of my parents as grandparents to my children, and finally of myself as a grandmother.

As I reflect on my own experience in this light I have come to see more clearly how the threads of social change have been inevitably interwoven with my own story, although I may not have registered it at the time.

MY GRANDMOTHERS

I was born with the outbreak of the Second World War. My father had come to England from Eire, as it then was, at the age of nineteen. My mother was English. He was thirty and she twenty when they married. It seems a long look back to my grandparents from where I am today.

My Irish grandmother had ten children, nine boys and a girl. My father came towards the end of the line. Incidentally, those ten children produced only five in the next generation, including my sister and myself, but that is part of the story of Ireland rather than of my personal story. Because of distance and the war I only saw this Granny once before she died and my memory, from the worm's eye view of a small child, is of a long black skirt and apron with black laced shoes sticking out beneath. My father's fluent stories of his childhood later on gave me some idea of the material harshness of her life and the sheer faith and fortitude required to live it.

My English grandmother had six children, my mother being number four. She had married late for her day and had also known economic hardship. I have no memory of her ever taking care of me or my older sister. It was rather our role to visit her and our grandfather and, particularly after his death, to perform little services for her. Towards the end of her life when I had left home she lived with my parents for some time. She loved to reminisce about hard times; for example the many times she pawned her wedding ring and gold bracelet when my grandfather was away in the Dardanelles in the First World War. But the stories were not all sad. Some were hair-raising, comical or 'saucy' and we were fond of her.

However, the idea then or earlier that she might have been a help or support to our mother never seemed to arise. It was only much later that I understood how lonely my mother had been during the war years when my father was away in the Navy, and I reflected with puzzlement on my grandmother's non-involvement. Her six children eventually produced thirteen grandchildren who mostly hardly knew each other and she never initiated family reunions or get-togethers.

What might have been large extended families on both sides somehow never materialised. Age, distance, family rifts are partial explanations. On the other hand my husband's extended family was an unusually close one. When we met I recognised that this was what I wanted for us. It is worth noting that the desire for closeness probably sprung from my mother-in-law's reaction to her own rather isolated childhood. She was an only child, sent early to boarding school while her parents spent many of her childhood years in India. So we took on, and passed on, a powerful family belief in closeness and solidarity. This has found expression in a remarkable degree of closeness in the geographical sense which probably makes our family, at its present state of evolution, atypical of its time.

My husband's parents and mine already lived quite near to us, but when my father retired in 1970 he and my mother moved into a house in our road. All our four adult children now live in the same area of London, including my daughter with our eighteen month old grand-daughter. My son and daughter-in-law, with our two grandsons, live in the next road. Is this apparent bucking of the social trend a subliminal reaction to the increasing disruption and vulnerability of family life as well as a deliberate choice, based on family history and values, for connection rather than separateness? Well, it also makes a lot of practical sense. Granny doesn't have to come and stay when she wants to visit the grandchildren!

A BLOODLESS REVOLUTION

Our children arrived in the late sixties and early seventies. My own parents and my husband's took to the role of grandparents with enthusiasm. They were pretty good at not interfering in our child-rearing methods. This must have been hard as they had raised their babies according to the harsh dicta of Dr. Truby King who was as far removed from the affable Dr. Spock as it is possible to be. Actually I have a hunch that few mothers really followed Truby King all the way. They had too much common sense. However Dr. Spock certainly represented a revolution in child-rearing manuals, and the advice handed out by today's writers is much closer to his in both spirit and detail than his was to Truby King's. No continuing revolution here, which makes harmonious grandparenting a lot easier than it was for our parents' generation. However, they gave the children a lot of love and affection and were involved and interested in their progress and activities. They were willing and generous babysitters. Perhaps they became less close to our children in their teenage years when values began to diverge and be challenged, though they were on the whole tolerant of the loud music, multiple earrings and other eccentricities of adolescence.

I am aware as a grandmother of trying to make a similar contribution to my children's families. In fact it was my late father who made the running. After retirement he was a tireless provider of school runs, held finishing tapes at Sports Days, was never too busy to tell stories, walk to the swings or babysit. As a consequence he had a remarkable relationship with my children until he died. Perhaps he was making up for the years of separation from his little girls during the war. The story goes that meeting my father as a toddler I said, "You're not my Daddy. My Daddy's in the Navy!"

What seemed so simple for my father was more complex for my mother. Like most of her generation, my mother never pursued a career. Marrying in 1936, she had two babies by the time that the Second World War (as the First had done in its day) made its contribution to a major revision of women's roles and aspirations. She was always ambivalent about my efforts to continue with education, training or part-time work as far as family responsibilities allowed. This was in spite of the fact that she had wholly supported my going to University and had always encouraged me to think in terms of a (preferably professional) career. What was unspoken was the assumption that marriage, to be delayed as long as possible, and certainly motherhood, would put an end to all that. I think she was in the end envious of the opportunities and support I enjoyed, although she contributed to them, and she became resentful of the constraints and limitations that had hedged her in as a woman and as a mother. Observing her two daughters as adults only increased her sense of the limitations of her own life. (This was very different for her younger sister who had determinedly escaped to independent life at the outbreak of war by joining the WAAF when my mother was already tied down with babies and alone.)

So I was lucky that, in no small measure due to the support of this older generation, I was able to bring up our children while continuing to study, train and then work at least part-time. It was not too difficult for me to hold on to and expand a life for myself outside the home as the children's needs became less all-consuming.

It was also in the earliest years of motherhood that I became aware of feminism as a developing force. I remember pushing the pram to the library and reading Simone de Beauvoir and Betty Friedan with a sense of exhilaration. I suppose I was from early on giving my daughters the implicit message that it is desirable and possible for women to combine a professional and family life, which was actually similar to the message I received from my mother. But just as my acting on the message turned out to be disturbingly different from my mother's ideas for me, so I am disturbed by the experience of so many of my daughters' generation as they act upon the messages transmitted by my own.

On a personal level I can see that although I often thought that I was 'having it all', in fact I was effectively cushioned by the financial security of my husband's earning power from the necessity of full-time, career-structured, well-rewarded employment. It is the successful combination of these elements with motherhood that count as 'having it all' today. This is a lot harder than anything I was attempting, even though it seemed quite 'modern' and ambitious to my own mother.

Perhaps in a similar way to hers, the experience of seeing my own children as parents has given me pause. The winds of the hurricane of social change are whirling around as their generation live the effects of the revolution to which I largely subscribed, but without shedding blood.

GUILT OF THE WORKING GRANNY

Blood is being shed by today's young women.

My elder daughter was fortunate to have six months maternity leave from her job as a magazine editor after her daughter's birth. But there was no possibility of adapting her working life on her return without serious threat to her career and so to her financial status, future security and so on. She and many of her friends combining work with childrearing would echo the view of Jan Wallcraft, Programme Manager of the Mental Health Foundation, recently quoted as saying, "Sadly for women, having it all means doing it all".[15] Moreover it has been their experience that it takes about 18 months from returning from maternity leave to retrieve the same measure of credibility and respect in the workplace enjoyed before embarking on it. This struggle usually involves avoiding all reference to child care issues, working long hours without demur and generally showing no evidence of the new situation apart from the bags under their eyes. A study published by the American Psychological Association comments on the sharply increasing incidence of depression among young women.[16] Their research indicates that this is not a biological problem to be treated with Prozac, but a sociological one of increased responsibilities combined with low social power. Though spared the horrors of depression, my daughter knows all about the torn emotions, frustration and stress of the working mother.

Which brings me to the issue of the guilt of the working granny. Having slowly built up a working life while my children grew up, their departure has meant a much greater commitment to work. How should I be balancing the demands of my own work with the needs of my children and grandchildren? I have reduced my work with clients quite considerably in order to be more available but it still feels hard to have to say, "Sorry, I'm working," if my daughter or daughter-in-law need help. My daughter-in-law has been able to choose to be a full-time mother and homemaker at the present time, so perhaps I feel less guilt in relation to her. But keeping a good connection and being a good grandmother to her children is equally important to me.

I am full of admiration for both my daughter and my daughter-in-law. Their lives are very different, yet on occasion each has had to deal with external pressures where their life style is questioned and criticised, my daughter by those who see her return to full-time work as selfish and damaging, and my daughter-in-law by those who see her commitment to domestic life as narrow and dependent.

Mothers today cannot please everyone in the flux and reflux of ideas around family life, although one of the more encouraging developments of recent years has been that they rarely feel the need to do so anymore. The right, if not always the confidence and support, to decide upon their own pattern of life seems largely won. However, they need to be very clear about their own values, and more than anything they need partners who share these values and are prepared to engage actively in creating the kind of couple and family life to which they both aspire.

REDISCOVERING THE FAMILY

This brings me to another concern for today's grandmothers. Both marriages and non-married partnerships are more vulnerable now. In part this is because of the high expectations placed upon the couple relationship since the revolution; expectations becoming demands for a high degree of collaboration, flexibility and maturity in both partners.

Young families need particular support, from grandparents among others, when relationships are stressed or even breaking down. What is more, when couples with young children split, grandmothers may find themselves at one or other extreme, either taking over a large part of responsibility for their grandchildren or sadly marginalised by the rift. I have friends in each of these situations.

Women have always needed the emotional and practical support they traditionally offer each other. I have the role of proxy grandmother to the four English grandchildren of my sister who lives in the United States. Grandmothers, mothers, sisters and daughters have a connection whose intensity can easily become conflictual, but which is a vital part of social cohesion and continuity. This connection, at a time of diversification of family patterns, where single parent families and blended families seem likely soon to outnumber the traditional nuclear family, will surely become even more vital to the continuity, stability and economic viability that children need in order to do well.

It is ironic that the outcome of the revolution may be to throw a new generation of families more and more back on the time-honoured resources of the extended family, in the context of a society still largely dominated by masculine values and which is itself prepared to make few concessions to the new circumstances brought about by social change. Here I think one should also take account of the workplace revolution, largely enacted in the eighties, which has brought about a severe decline in job security, and a workforce that labours for the longest hours in Europe. These additional burdens make adjustment to the changes in family life and the role of women even more difficult. Social policies designed to help the family need to look at these aspects of working life as well as being much more responsive to the needs of working women.

In fact one unforeseen outcome of the revolution may be that we have focused unduly on the lives of women and children without taking enough account of the total family picture. As the mother and grandmother of sons and grandsons I am every bit as concerned about the balance of their lives between the demands of work, family and personal needs as I am about my daughters and grand-daughter. There is also a need for enquiry into the effects of the social and work revolutions on the lives of grandfathers, fathers and sons as they are confronted by the changed expectations of the women in their lives and an increasingly unstable and demanding working environment.

At the turn of the century social and economic change have put a huge additional strain on families, to the extent that the family has often needed to redefine itself in more generous and flexible ways. The ability of the family to do just that is one of its greatest strengths, and families need to be encouraged to look beyond traditional boundaries to provide all members with the support and nurture they need. Grandparents - and some children may wind up with several sets - can have an important role to play, especially with the expectation of a longer and fitter span of life. Where grandparents are absent, some primary schools have adopted local 'grannies' to support individual children as helpers and friends. Although there are some signs of a pendulum swing (more structured child-rearing practices for example) the changes wrought by the revolution cannot be reversed. It will take all the considerable resources of families across generations to minimise the potentially damaging effect of disruption on today's grandchildren.

It will also demand a continuing serious assessment of the impact of social and economic policies on the vulnerable fabric of family life. If I am personally aware of real stresses as a grandmother in a comfortably-off, united, middle-class family, I am equally aware how much more painfully these same stresses impact on families in less favoured circumstances.

ON BEING A GRANDMOTHER

Tessa Blackstone

RECEIVING THE NEWS

During a performance at Covent Garden of *Rheingold*, the first opera in Wagner's Ring Cycle, I was called out of the Box where I was sitting with my guests, by a member of the Opera House staff. He told me my son wanted to speak to me on the telephone. "It's a girl," Ben told me. "She has got red hair and she's really beautiful." I can think of no telephone call in my life that made me so happy. I returned to my seat feeling intense joy and unable to resist whispering to my friends, "I've just heard I have a grand-daughter." I will never be able to listen to *Rheingold* again without re-living that moment of extraordinary happiness.

When I went to the hospital the next day I was overwhelmed by my son and daughter-in-law's delight at becoming parents. Their emotions dominated mine and brought back clear memories of the intense emotion I felt in the first days of my elder child's life. Since the family of my daughter-in-law Suzi lived in Dublin and Los Angeles she and Ben

Tessa Blackstone has been Minister of State for Education and Employment *since May 1997. Before that she was* Master of Birkbeck College *and opposition spokesperson on Foreign Affairs in the* House of Lords. *She has three grand-daughters, Scarlet born in 1991 and Amber and Ruby, identical twins, born in 1994. In November 1998 she summed up for the government in a Lords debate on grandparenting.*

brought the baby to stay with me for a few days when she left hospital twenty-four hours after the birth.

SHARING THE ANXIETIES

Real grandmotherhood then began when on the second night the baby, now with the name of Scarlet, would not feed and would not stop crying either. My advice was sought at midnight but nothing I suggested worked. Scarlet was inconsolable and I was inept, indeed useless. We called the midwife and peace and happiness was eventually restored. But at least I was able to share the anxiety that new parents feel at such times and try to provide reassurance that there was nothing seriously wrong with her.

Scarlet is now eight and a half and has identical twin sisters, Amber and Ruby, who are just six. They live in London, less than twenty minutes drive away. So whilst there are other reasons preventing me from seeing them very frequently, geographical distance is not a problem. The main difficulty, as for many young grandmothers I suspect, is that my job is a barrier. Since it involves long hours, including work in the evenings and at weekends, I am not as available as I would like to be. But before recounting my relationship with them, and how I feel as a grandmother today, I need to go back a little.

The circumstances of Amber and Ruby's birth were not straightforward and happy as in Scarlet's case; indeed they were traumatic. When my daughter-in-law Suzi's pregnancy was in the twenty-eighth week she started to bleed heavily and was admitted to hospital. After a night of indecision and uncertainty about whether to intervene the obstetricians eventually decided to do a caesarean section. Sick with fear, I went to the hospital to be with Ben and waited outside the theatre with him.

Two teams of paediatricians were on hand in the theatre to rush the babies into intensive care. The medical teams emerged in turn with the babies in portable incubators and congratulated my son as they vanished into the lift, telling him they were both girls. Fearing that he might be disappointed not to have a boy, I hugged Ben and said how lovely it would be to have all these girls and to be looked after by them in his old age. He then broke down and wept tears of joy, saying he had always wanted three daughters!

I suspect after the tension of the previous twenty-four hours he was weeping with relief that these little mites, weighing in at 2lbs 9ozs and 2lbs 10ozs, were actually alive. But the next two weeks were to prove enormously testing as they struggled for life against the odds. They survived as a result of the skill and care of the staff in the premature baby unit at University College Hospital. Grandmothers in these circumstances cannot provide any direct care. But they can help with an older sibling, and give as much as possible in the way of psychological support. Suzi virtually lived at the hospital for seven weeks, going through many ups and downs before the twins were strong enough to leave.

One member of the family who appeared to survive the stress without being affected was their elder sister Scarlet. She took the wired-up miniature babies and the machinery that surrounded them in her stride and seemed on the surface to accept her mother's absence from home. However, one week-end it became clear that she too was finding life difficult. I took her to visit my brother and his three children then aged nearly eight, five and fifteen months.

When I was out of sight in the house and everyone else's back was turned in the garden she bit the baby, who screamed piteously. This led to serious scolding of Scarlet by the baby's mother, at which Scarlet ran sobbing into the house in search of Granny. Her act of aggression was out of character, but not hard to explain. She had had enough of babies and found an accessible victim, where she could demonstrate her feelings! My job was to console her, then apologise to my sister-in-law and leave.

By leaving I could give her the undivided attention, away from babies of any age or size, that she obviously craved.

When she was a baby and toddler I frequently looked after Scarlet on a Friday or Saturday night, so that Ben and Suzi could go out. I kept a cot at my house where she could sleep, together with some familiar toys and books to play with and look at. The bonding process was completed early. I did not have the same opportunities with Amber and Ruby. Within the same family the experience of grandparenting can be very different, and I am certainly a case in point. Because they were so tiny and delicate the twins required a great deal of care and attention. Their exhausted parents needed full-time help at home in the shape of a nanny, and when Suzi returned to work an au pair too, to share the burden. It is hard to contemplate, let alone fully understand the demands made by premature twins without experiencing them. It is compounded when there is an older child too, who is under three.

There could be no question of bringing them to stay with me for a Friday night as Scarlet had done. It was too much effort to transport two babies and all their clobber plus a three year old from one house to another. Early on I offered to go to them instead. The offer was accepted. But I singularly failed to live up to expectations. Having given me all the instructions I needed about feeding the babies, and a contact number in case I needed it, Ben and Suzi went off for their much-needed night off.

After an hour or two my troubles began. One of the babies woke up and cried. I made up a bottle and settled down to feed her. Then the other baby woke up and cried too. I put down the first baby, who bellowed with rage, and I went down several flights of stairs to the basement kitchen to make up a bottle for the second baby. When I came back I attempted to feed both babies together as demonstrated by my daughter-in-law. But by then the first baby was in such a state about her interrupted feed that she refused to go back to it. While trying to placate her by walking her around the room – checking whether she was suffering from wind – I had to put down the second baby, who then screamed even louder at being put down and denied her bottle. The combined hullabaloo finally woke up the elder sister, who started crying too. So I found myself running from one child to another, not knowing which one to give precedence to, and wishing I were a Hindu God with three sets of arms.

In the middle of all this Suzi rang to ask whether everything was all right. "No," I wailed, "I can't cope, you'll have to come home." She was astounded. "You can't cope; I can't believe it," she said. The image she had of me as the coping professional woman apparently had extended to the coping Granny until that moment - when I suspect it vanished for ever. When Ben and Suzi arrived back they teased me for being inadequate, and inadequate I certainly felt in a rueful kind of way. Fortunately, however, I recovered from this failure and partly restored my reputation on later baby-sitting occasions.

Incidents like this apart, being a grandmother has undoubtedly been one of the greatest pleasures of my life. And until it happened I would never have anticipated the happiness it has brought me. Most of us love our children. I certainly do. But while we are bringing them up they make us suffer. It is physically hard work when they are small and emotionally testing especially when they are adolescents.

Perhaps not all grandparents love their grand-children with the intensity that they love their children, though I suspect that many do. But grandchildren do not make their grandparents suffer because in most cases grandparents do not have the day-to-day responsibility for bringing them up and for trying to turn them from naughty children into nice adults. The unique nature of the relationship is that it is one based on love without the disadvantages that other such relationships bring -

whether as in rivalry between siblings, misunderstandings as between close friends, jealousy as between lovers, irritation and boredom as between spouses.

CHANGES IN GRANDPARENTS' ROLES

This book is about grandmothers rather than grandfathers. Is there a difference? There clearly was between my grandparents when I look back to my own childhood. Following the normal statistical pattern both my grandfathers died at a significantly younger age than my grandmothers. I don't remember my father's father who died when I was two, and I hardly remember my mother's father who was a remote and rather distant figure and who died when I was ten. Both my grandmothers lived many years longer – long enough to become great-grandmothers and take pleasure in my children. My grand-daughters in turn never knew one of their grandfathers; my ex-husband died of cancer at the age of forty-four. Without succumbing to spiritualism I have occasionally wished I could talk to him and tell him about the grand-daughters he never saw.

But when men survive long enough to be grandfathers, do they have a different relationship to their grandchildren? In that men traditionally have taken less responsibility for the care of children, the answer is 'yes'. But as gender differences diminish in the care of children, it is 'no'. I know more than one recently retired grandfather who is spending part of each week looking after a grandchild, and one who even took early retirement to do so. Such cases are still unusual, but there will be more of them. And even if relatively few men take on this degree of responsibility, as men live longer and the gap between male and female longevity diminishes more grandchildren will have a different experience to mine and will get to know and love their grandfathers. They in turn will relate to their grandchildren in similar ways to grandmothers. Old men will be able to become 'new men'!

The revolution in patterns of employment for women, which has seen even the mothers of young children working outside the home in very large numbers, offers some opportunities for grandparents to help their children by caring for their grandchildren. But geographical mobility and the working patterns of older women in their fifties and early sixties, who are increasingly themselves employed full-time, both restrict the scope for this. Paradoxically those who become grandparents later, after normal retirement age, may be able to spend more time helping to care for their grandchildren than younger grandmothers - as long as they are not too old.

There is perhaps an optimum period to be an active grandparent, for working women, between around sixty to seventy-five - before fatigue and decrepitude start getting in the way. And they certainly will. Even younger grandmothers, who may be - and indeed should be - a little more indulgent than parents, often breathe a sigh of relief when the parents turn up to take the children home, and the mess all over the house can be cleared up and tranquillity restored. Looking after small children *is* tiring for older people.

Being a grandparent is not just a continuation of parenting, except when grandparents take over the care of their grandchildren full-time and in doing so become substitute parents. As a grandmother I do not believe I can be the source of unconditional love that parenting involves, nor the figure of authority and disburser of discipline, nor the purveyor of moral values.

Children are socialised by their parents, not their grandparents. That does not mean, however, that grandparents have no influence. They *can* influence their grandchildren both directly and indirectly. They can tell their grandchildren about their own beliefs and values as they start to grow up. And while they are small they can, in day-to-day matters like sharing toys, putting things away when they have finished with them and eating what they have been given, exert some influence over their behaviour. What they cannot do, however, unless they have longer term responsibility for their care, is impose sanctions and institute punishment. That is for parents. For grandparents to do it would undermine their special relationship with grandchildren.

Indirect influence comes in a variety of ways, from providing role models for younger generations to advising their children about how to bring up their offspring. I believe that young people do observe their grandparents and often unconsciously as much as consciously will model themselves on them in certain respects. My daughter's deep love of children and special way in relating to them at their own level is, I believe, modelled on my mother-in-law who behaved in the same way herself with children. Equally, my maternal grandmother passed on to me, not genetically but through my observation of her, a sort of orderliness in organising her day that amounted to more than tidiness. It was perhaps more akin to careful planning of her time.

KNOWING THE RANGE AND LIMITS

How much we should say to our children about how they ought to bring up their children is and always has been tricky, and is of course the subject of many mother-in-law stories and jokes. The interfering Granny is not a happy spectacle, although when terrible mistakes are being made it is hard to hold back. It is always fortunate, as in my own case, when the basic approach to parenting adopted by our children matches our own views. One of the pleasures of being a grandmother is to be asked advice about what to do. And it is usually best to wait to be asked, rather than offering it gratuitously. Certainly we are more likely to be asked if we hold back when we are *not* asked! In general it probably pays to be fairly laid back and not too insistent about a particular approach or solution.

Although I am writing here in a personal and anecdotal way, the social scientist in me can't help asking what we

actually know from systematic academic studies about the role
of grandmothers at the end of the twentieth century. I suspect
that it is precious little. Not much research seems to have been
done on the subject, in spite of the fact that estimates suggest
there are 16.5 million grandparents in Britain, and that most of
them see their grandchildren fairly regularly.

In the USA more work has been done. What emerges from
it seems to be that it is dangerous to generalise about what
grandparenthood means today. There is clearly now a great
diversity in styles and roles. In some cases the relationship is
formal and distant. In others it may involve taking actual
responsibility for the child or children. In yet others it is all
about treats and having fun. Similar levels of heterogeneity
presumably apply here.

What would be interesting to know is whether there are
particular patterns of grandparenting behaviour associated with
different social groups, or with personality types, or with
earlier experiences as a parent. For example we know little
about class differences. Nor do we know how such differences
are shaped by circumstances such as the span of a generation.
Working class families have been traditionally characterised by
earlier marriage and younger parenthood, leading to narrower
generations than in middle or upper middle class families and
affecting the age at which people become grandparents. Such
class differences may be less great today as the trend towards
later marriage continues and spreads.[17]

Nor do we know much about trends over time, though one
recent study in the UK undertaken by the *Family Policy
Studies Centre* found that levels of contact with grandparents
had fallen greatly over the last decade.[18] These findings
prompted the researchers to consider whether younger and
more affluent grandparents now want to be freer from family
responsibilities.

If these findings were replicated by other studies, should it
be a matter for regret that levels of contact are declining? I
believe it should. Given the stressful nature of being a parent,

grandparents can be helpful stress-buffers in difficult times. High levels of divorce and separation cannot necessarily be reduced by the support of grandparents. But their continued help and care may at least do something to mitigate the effects. More positively it would be a pity if geographical distance, and the enjoyment by increasingly affluent grandparents of holidays abroad and a wider range of leisure pursuits led to them miss out on the great pleasure to be derived from regular contact with their grandchildren. Surely these need not be mutually exclusive.

LOOKING TO THE FUTURE

For my own part, as a youngish grandparent I look forward to the delight of watching my grandchildren grow up, reading their school reports, learning about their successes and their struggles, spending time with them and talking to them about what interests them as well as me, learning from them about the changing world with which they will be more in touch than I. And although I know I must not count chickens before they hatch, one day I look forward to being a great-grandmother too. My fantasy photograph for the year 2025 has me sitting in the middle of a family photograph with my middle-aged children on either side of me, my beautiful grand-daughters, by then mature women in their thirties, behind me and their children sitting at my feet with the youngest of them - a baby - on my lap.

WHERE HAVE THE NEIGHBOURS GONE?

Linda Whelan

When I had my kids we lived in streets that were real communities. Members of families used to live near each other, and had a lot of friends in the same streets too. We all used to know each other well, and our children would play together outside. My mum would look after my kids a lot, but the neighbours would help keep an eye on them too and we would do the same with theirs. It was like a big family. Everybody helped each other.

But now I am a grandma myself it is not like that anymore. There have been so many changes that sometimes I wonder how it is all going to end. Grandmothers still do a lot, but these days there is a lot of pressure on them, and difficulties, and many don't have the time to do much.

NOBODY HAS ANY TIME

Nowadays most grandmothers still have their own jobs. I only gave up mine because I couldn't manage anymore, and even that has not meant I can look after my grandchildren more often because my mother is now housebound and I have to do the shopping and cooking for her as well. The only grandparents I know who have stopped work so they can help

---

Linda Whelan lives in north London close to her housebound mother and fairly near to her four children - three daughters and one son. She has five grandchildren through her daughters. Two years ago she gave up her job office-cleaning because of heart problems.

out are where there are single parents. If they see a daughter struggling by herself they may feel that they have to step in.

There are so many single parents these days, and quite a few of them actually live with their own parents. A cousin of mine for example has a daughter like this, who has got to go back to work soon after her maternity leave finishes. She has to go back or else she will have to return her maternity leave money. In my day the state would pay for the maternity, and not the firm. One of the reasons so many women go back to work is because they've got good jobs and need the money. So my cousin looks after the baby and her daughter has gone back to work.

Another thing is that lots of mothers do not like to use childcare. I know that my daughters would not trust anyone to look after their kids. So I have them when they go out. And if I don't then they won't go out. Or if it comes to it my mum will look after them. But she is quite old now, she is seventy-seven and she can't really do much. She only lives down the road, so the kids are sometimes dropped off after school. But she can't take much, and does not like all the noise they make.

I know that lots of grannies feel that they are being taken for a ride by their daughters. Someone I used to work with spends a lot of time helping to look after her grandchildren. Her daughter is not married, and has quite an important office job. She just assumed that if she had children her mother would take care of them for her. She didn't ask. She had two children close together and stopped work for a few months when they were very small. But each time afterwards she just said that she was going back to work and her mother, Jennie, could look after them for her.

My friend, Jennie, felt that her daughter's work was more important than her own, and that the most valuable thing she could do was to help her out. So she left her own job and spends almost all her time now looking after her two grandchildren. They stay with her most nights during the week and she takes them to playgroup and school and collects them afterwards. She takes them to parties and on outings. And she is the person that teachers talk to if there are any problems.

Jennie loves her grandchildren and wants to do the best she can for them, even though she is very tired and doesn't get much break from them. What makes her resentful is that her daughter is always grumbling at her and never seems to be satisfied with what she does. When her daughter goes on holiday with the children, or takes them on an outing herself, she never invites her mother along. And she gets very annoyed if Jennie suggests that the children's father might like to see them sometimes - though she knows that he *has* met them and would like to be in touch with them. I don't know how they will ever sort it out.

CHILDREN DON'T BEHAVE

On top of all that, children themselves are different to how they used to be. I don't know if it's because so many of them live in flats now. The children go to school and they come home but that is it. They don't really play outside these days. They stay in and then are very unruly and noisy. It's not just my own grandchildren who are like that. I think that parents today are not strict with their children. So you end up giving in to them yourself, just to shut them up.

I think that it has a lot to do with whether the dad is around or not. Some of them are here one day and gone the next. That is confusing for them. And families are not bringing the kids up properly; they've got no respect for older people. When you tell seven-year-olds not to do something they'll go and do it again, and swear at you. They swear so much and they're just little kids really.

There is no authority now, and a lot of the problem starts at school. There's no authority at school as the teachers can't discipline them, and then when they come home their parents are not involved enough and just let them get away with it there too.

I have tried to be fully involved with my grandchildren. When the first was born I was there at the hospital. I didn't see the birth but I held him within the first fifteen minutes. It's been more or less like that with them all, except for the last one, when I was a bit late. I have been there at the hospital pretty much as it took place. The Dads have been happy to let me hold them. Dads usually get possessive over their little ones, especially their first. But they have all let me hold theirs - even before them sometimes.

It all felt very much like it was with my own children, and that feeling has remained. So now if I want to tell my grandchildren off, or smack them, I can. It's like they are mine. My mum was the same with my kids. It's a sort of tradition. Going back a bit, my grandmother used to hit me and she used to look after me a lot too. So I think that is why we're like we are. Some grandmothers feel like they're not really involved in the family. They feel a bit useless. Or they don't like to interfere. But it's not like that in our family. The grandmother has quite a strong place.

FAMILIES ARE BEING SPLIT

The other thing is that lots of families round here are getting broken up by their housing. We can't get together so easily these days because we can't live so close any more. I have to stay here as my mother needs me for her shopping and cleaning. But my children are going to have to move to get more bedrooms for their children, and they won't be able to find flats in this area because of all the Asian immigrants who are coming here now. My children will have to move out, and I won't be able to go on looking after their children.

The grandmother role is still very important. Perhaps it is even more so than in my mum's time. The main problem for me is the way that the community is changing. This is not just the new immigrants themselves, but also to do with the fact that a lot of families are now mixed race. The parents don't get married, mainly because they are not accepted by each other's families. Marriage in itself is not important, but it is good to have two people together to share the responsibility for children. And with mixed race parents this often does not seem to work out. They can't get help from their own parents during difficult times, and then often enough don't stay together themselves for very long.

It has all started to fall apart around here. Some families are close, but they aren't the same as they used to be, and they aren't part of a neighbourhood any more. In my day we had Sunday Schools and Guides and things like that where our children could get to know others in the area. It still happens like this perhaps if you live outside London, but it is not like that here. These traditions are just not there any more, and it is too late to save them. The housing has altered everything, because families can't live near each other any more. They split families up, and move other people in.

It's a way of life they shouldn't have changed.

A GRANDMOTHER DISPOSSESSED

Aileen Flanagan

EARLY DAYS

I can't say that I was very pleased when my first grand-daughter was born. My son Douglas was very young and had not been together with his girlfriend for very long. They had not planned it, and were not ready for that sort of commitment. Douglas was working as a hairdresser. He had just fully qualified, and had become the manager of a hairdressers and was working very long hours and was not around for long enough to give Cheryl much help in looking after Susie. So we could see problems ahead.

We had pretended to be pleased of course, as what had happened could not be changed. My husband's first reaction had been that they should go and get married. We were brought up in Catholic homes and were taught to respect marriage and all that. And so when our son got his girlfriend pregnant Fergal immediately said, "Quick, get them down to the church," almost adding, "Where's the brimstone?" I talked him out of it.

They did not really want to get married, and I wouldn't have wanted them to do it for us. They would have resented it. I thought about it and decided, "No, let's not push them

---

Aileen Flanagan is a shop manager in Coventry, where she lives with her husband Fergal. She has two sons, and one daughter, and two grand-daughters through her older son Douglas.

together for us, it has got to be only if they want to do it."
And in fact I was right. They did not stay together for long.

At first everything seemed great. I was actually at the birth
which was exciting and nice. And when she came out of
hospital they came to stay with us for about a week or two –
so right from the early stages I was with them and spent a lot
of time with them. Cheryl's parents lived down in Liverpool,
so I was more like a parent to her. I was supporting her like
a mother. I would offer to babysit whenever they wanted it, so
they could go out for the night, and just tried to make things
as easy for them as I could. One time when she stayed with
her mother for a while I went to Liverpool to meet her and she
was there with lots of grandchildren. Cheryl came from a
family of seven, and her mother seemed to love being
surrounded by children and grandchildren, and everything was
fine between her and Cheryl. I am a different sort of
grandmother. I would not want to be a full-time grandmother,
bringing up grandchildren and doing all that all over again.
Not long after that Cheryl's mum became ill and died and I
had to support her all the more then because I was the only
mother she had left.

None of this lasted for very long. I blame Douglas for a lot
of this. He was not good in a family situation. He loved to
work and then enjoy himself, and did not have much time to
be with Susie and Cheryl. He's a workaholic, who then likes
to go out and enjoy himself. He provides material things, but
that's not what it's all about. Spending time with people is
more important, because it means that relationships can grow
strong.

Cheryl was not much better. He was earning a lot, but she
was spending it as soon as he was earning it. She seemed
happy to give up her job as a receptionist as soon as she
became pregnant, and liked to be at home. However she was
not the kind of person you could join in things and give advice
to. You had to think twice before saying anything to her. Even
with things like, "Oh, the straps should be on the baby when

she's in the pram," you knew that you should bite your tongue and keep quiet. Even little things like that. Maybe it was because it was her first baby, but she became quite possessive. If my husband came into the room and made a noise it would be "Shh!", and "Don't pick her up." There wasn't a relaxed feeling about it all. So things were quite difficult altogether, and the relationship was rather on and off for about three years.

Fergal thought that it would help if we set them up in business. At one stage he wanted to find them a hairdressers in Liverpool. But I didn't think that they were mature enough. I could see that they weren't very responsible, and talked him out of it. That didn't go down very well, of course, and they didn't speak to me for about three months afterwards because they knew I had stopped him. But I felt that I was doing the right thing at the time. They didn't value money properly, and weren't responsible with it, and I didn't feel that they were ready for it.

LOSING TOUCH

Then she started to get friendly with my son's best friend, and one day she just went to live with him. And that was the end of that really. She saw me for a while, and then didn't want to go on with that either. Douglas felt very badly about it, because it was his best friend it was too much for him. But he left her alone, as I was the one doing all the contact. I went on sending her birthday cards and Christmas cards and so on; but after a while she just returned them. She just wanted to break the ties altogether, and start a new life. I did not resent it at first as I knew that she felt bitter with my son. I thought that if she got over that she would let us see them sometimes, especially as I had had so much contact with her at the beginning. But I did feel a bit hurt.

Since then I have struggled to try and stay in touch. It is the in-laws who suffer most when parents break up. It started to get really difficult around Susie's fourth birthday. I was driving along near where she lived and I saw them on the pavement. I stopped the car and got out to say hello to Susie, and Cheryl had another baby with her. And she said hello, very politely, and then, "I must go." I asked if I could make an arrangement to see Susie and she said something like, "You didn't want to know when you did see her." It was a silly comment to make, and I said, "You know it wasn't like that." But I didn't want to have an argument in the street, so I left them. Then later that day she actually went to get a court injunction against me, and told lots of lies about how I'd followed Susie through the school and how I'd threatened to take her to Ireland.

After that some people came around to give me a summons to court. I was shocked, and they came in and sat down and said that the judge could tell from the statement that it wasn't true. So I agreed to go to court. It was the first time I'd been in court, so I went along on my own. I didn't want any of the family involved. The judge was very fair and said that he would never deny the right of a grandparent to see a grandchild. And he organised for us to meet with the court welfare officer to sort things out.

We arranged that I would see Susie in the holidays, in her own home. We tried that for a while, but Cheryl didn't make it comfortable for me. She'd sit there for the whole hour. The first time was the best. Susie came over to me and did a drawing. The times after that Cheryl would sit there showing her videos, and the child would hardly say anything and would never ask me any questions. It is natural for children to ask questions all the time, so that was odd. It was as if she had been programmed what to say, and what not to say. Cheryl told her not to call me granny, she was to call me Aileen. She would say that her new nanna bought her presents, as if that is what she was told to say. There's not a lot I could have done, and eventually they moved and didn't leave a forwarding address.

I have often thought that I could go back to the court and get them to look her up, because leaving a forwarding address was one of the conditions of the agreement. But I don't know if it's the right thing to do. It might disrupt her family life. I'd love to see her, but it might make her unsettled. I don't know whether it's right, or whether it is just selfish of me. As a grandparent I have rights, but I have to balance these with what is right for the child. I've been worrying over it for years. I still don't know whether to go back to court or not. And Susie is growing up now, she is twelve years old.

LIVING IN A SHADOW

Susie may have forgotten about me now. But when she is older she may want to know where she came from. I think that children have the right to know who their natural relations are. I just hope the same thing doesn't happen with my other grandchild. It does not seem very likely, but you never know how things may turn out. Douglas has done the same thing again, with a different partner. That new relationship broke up about a year ago, and for the same sort of reasons. Douglas would say that it was because his new partner Marianne suffered from depression. But I would say that he did not do anything to change the mistakes he made previously. One of his friends owns a restaurant/pub, and he likes to go round there and enjoy himself. He just isn't a family person.

However I feel that I have a more secure tie with Phoebe than I did with Susie. Marianne is different altogether. She says that I can see Phoebe any day, and she's happy if I have her to stay. She is two now, nearly three, and I often have her for the weekend and Marianne says that she will never stop me from seeing her. She phones me, and visits, and Phoebe calls me 'granny'. It is a different situation altogether. I hope that she sticks to it, because as time goes on she might meet someone else and the same might happen again. You can never tell. So I can't help feeling insecure about it.

The whole thing has made me rather wary of Douglas and his relationships. I have said to him that when he gets a new girlfriend now he will have to tell them about what he has done in the past, and if he does not then I will. I don't want to have to get to know another girlfriend and suddenly find that she's not there. And I wouldn't want another grandchild to feel like I was only going to see them for a few weeks and then not see them. I would advise any girl who meets him what he's like – that he's not really a homemaker. He says he's never going to be one for the pipe and slippers. The girls should know. What they see is what they will get.

Even Fergal now finds it hard with any relationships Douglas makes. It's hard because we get to know these very nice girls and they become part of the family. But you can't get close to them as you don't know whether its going to be permanent. It has affected my daughter, too. She says she doesn't want children. She would rather adopt or foster children, to give unwanted children a home. She finds it hard to get on with her brother's girlfriends, as she's afraid that she may lose contact. She did get close to her niece, and now she doesn't want to get involved with any more of her brother's relationships.

A GRANDMOTHER'S LOT

The younger generation does things quite differently these days, and lots of other grandmothers I talk to say that this makes life harder for them. Even down to how children are allowed to behave. They don't have a set bed time or a routine, and parents don't like you to stop them touching things or doing as they please. Often I see infants running along the street, when I would have had them on reins. A granny will often get called an 'interfering mother-in-law' if she makes any comment. But then they are expected to help out, especially by working mothers. And people don't stay together these days. More and more marriages are breaking up, and girls having babies younger and younger; and when they don't want to continue their relationships the whole family has to step in to help out. Children may come back home if a relationship breaks down. They start wanting to go out to parties and all that and the grandparents are left to look after the children. Young people are having children without thinking of the consequences. It seems glamorous, but I don't think it is. They don't think about how it is bound to change their lives.

There is a lot of pressure on grandparents to look after children, especially by working mothers. Grandparents feel that they have to do it. It is a guilt thing. Unless you have a career of your own it is difficult to say no. You are expected to have the children come over, and stay at the weekends. If you're not working yourself that is fine. But I am, and I don't want to spend all my time off looking after the grandchildren. But I have often had to step in with my youngest. Douglas would phone and say Marianne is having a nervous breakdown or something so could I take Phoebe. And I've done it because it is an emergency. He could easily have taken time off work to do it himself. But he thinks, "Oh, mum's job is not as important as mine." So I have to step in.

There are some full-time grandmothers I know who live near their grandchildren and help out a lot. One of my friends at church was saying how she takes her grandchildren to school, and looks after them again afterwards, while her children are at work. And it is tiring, as you are more protective when it is your grandchildren than with your own children. They are someone else's children, but your responsibility. You would not want anything bad to happen while you're looking after someone else's children. If you have the time, you can manage that. But if you are working, and trying to keep your own family and marriage together, then it is too much. I am exhausted by the end of a working day.

Years ago women of my age would not have worked, but now many have jobs *and* a social life of their own too. My children have to make an appointment to see me. I feel that in many ways I am much more in tune with my children and grandchildren than with my grandmother and even my mother. Fergal's mother, my mother-in-law, lived in Ireland so she didn't have much to do with her grandchildren, and did not see them growing up. My mother had four children and she loved having them and their children around her. She made herself a bit of a slave to the home. She had a lot of time for children, and would do anything for them - even give them a cigarette or a drink just to spoil them. She was always there for us. I hope that I am the same with mine.

I do try to detach myself a bit more and not get bogged down by worry, though. My mother used to get very stressed. Whereas my children off-load onto me all the time, my mother made herself ill with worry – especially over my brother's relationships. She could not cope. My brother is a lot like my eldest son, because he had several relationships and has got several children by different partners. It is as if my son has followed a pattern. My mother worried so much about the failed marriages. She used to talk about it all the time and worry if she could do anything. I thought to myself that this was something I would never do. It doesn't help your children if you are sitting in tears all the time. It is going to make them feel guilty for coming to you for help. You have to stay calm and listen. Sometimes that is all people want.

Fergal always accuses me of being too laid back when it comes to relationships and my children. But, I ask myself, what can I do? Look at the Queen's children. They are all split up, and it is not for lack of money. I suppose that people do break up a bit too easily now. They don't try to get through the rough patches, basically because they are selfish. People need to try a bit harder to keep families together. I think that because so many people are working all the time they don't have time for family life. People just think of themselves. They are out for what they can get. It is harder to give time now. Or maybe they don't want to give much time any more.

OUR CHANGING LIVES

Jan Pahl

"You don't look like a grandmother," they say. As tactfully as I can I reply that I do look like a grandmother; it is the picture of a grandmother inside their heads which has to be adjusted. The new grandmother of today does not have a bag of knitting and an apron; she has a briefcase and a mobile phone and hurries from her office to help with bath and bedtime. The new grandmother of today does not sit at home waiting to be visited: she finds a holiday bargain on the Internet and flies off around the world to return with exotic presents for her beloved grandchildren. The only thing which has not changed at all is the abiding love which grandmothers have for their grandchildren.

In this chapter I want to look at the changing lives of grandmothers, using objective evidence about demographic and social change and subjective evidence from my own experience as grandmother of Isabel, Barney and Molly, aged ten, eight and two, and of a baby due in five months time. Both types of evidence, however, must be regarded with some suspicion. The increasing diversity of family life, with more lone parents, more cohabiting couples, and more divorce and re-marriage, means that it is dangerous to make generalisations about family

Jan Pahl is Professor of Social Policy at the University of Kent at Canterbury. *Her books include* Private Violence and Public Policy, Money and Marriage, *and* Invisible Money: Family Finances in the Electronic Economy. *She has three children and three grandchildren, with another grandchild expected soon.*

life. In a multi-cultural society 'family life' takes a variety of different forms; and one's own experience is inevitably partial. In addition, much of what I will say could also apply to grandfathers, or to grandparents in general, but given the focus of this book, grandmothers are my main concern. In order to set the scene I begin by considering some of the demographic changes which have shaped the experience of grandmothers over the past century.

BALANCING WORK AND CHILDREN

A hundred years ago larger families and a shorter expectation of life meant that when they became grandmothers many women were still rearing their own children and were approaching old age themselves. Fifty years ago most married women were not in paid employment, so grandmothers were financially dependent on their husbands, while mothers were full-time parents.

The changes in the last quarter of the twentieth century mean that from a historical perspective the lives of today's grandmothers are unprecedented. Having had relatively small families, typically when they were in their twenties, and with an expectation of life approaching eighty, today's grandmothers can look forward to a lengthy span of active life after the birth of their first grandchild. The assumption that women will be in paid work has given them confidence and financial independence, while the high rate of employment among mothers means that grandmothers are valued for their contribution to child care.

So grandmothers can find themselves balancing work and family just as parents do. For example, last week I went straight from a meeting with the Vice-Chancellor at the University of Kent to a meeting with my grand-daughter at the Thumbelina nursery school. At the first meeting I was there in my capacity as Head of Department and we discussed the question of the Research Assessment Exercise. At the other I was there as 'Ganny', and as we ambled home we discussed the question of why pigeons fly away when you run after them. Both meetings demanded a variety of different skills and both expected good time keeping and my full attention. I like to think that I managed both without any of the participants being aware of my other commitments on that day.

The contribution which grandmothers make to child care varies according to the employment and marital status of the child's mother, as well as of the grandmother. One survey showed that where mothers are in full time employment twenty percent of grandparents, most of them grandmothers, look after the child during the day at least once a week. This proportion rises to thirty-two percent when the mother is in part time employment, but falls to fifteen percent when she is not in paid work. However, the proportion of grandparents looking after their grandchild at least once a week soars to fifty-six per cent when the child's parents are not together, underlining the important role which grandparents play when couples split up. There is a great discrepancy between the experience of the maternal and paternal grandparents, with the maternal grandparents increasing their involvement when parents divorce, while the paternal grandparents risk losing touch with their grandchildren altogether. [19]

The estrangement which can occur between grandchildren and grandparents when parents split up has been the cause of much unhappiness among grandparents. The Grandparents' Federation was set up in order to support those who, for one reason or another, have lost touch with their grandchildren or have become responsible for looking after them full time.[20] The Federation began in 1987, at a time when grandparents had no legal right with regard to their grandchildren. However, since the Children Act of 1989 grandparents can be 'named' in residence and contact orders. This can be very important when parental relationships break down or when children are accommodated by the local authority or placed with foster parents.

MAKING THE RELATIONSHIP WORK

Parents are crucial in mediating the relationship between grandmothers and grandchildren. Children pick up very quickly on the clues which their parents provide about the social world in which they live. A dismissive tone of voice when Granny is mentioned, an unsmiling face when she arrives, or eyes rolled towards the ceiling when she is talking, can all play their part in undermining the relationship. However, I am lucky. When I knock at the door of my grandchildren's house and hear my daughter or my son-in-law calling out joyfully, "Granny's here, Granny's here," I am deeply grateful to them for the part which they have played in making my relationship with their children such a happy one.

However, there is little on this topic in books of guidance for parents. When I became a grandmother I hurried out to buy Penelope Leach's book *Baby and Child* (1989), since I wanted to know the current norms of child-rearing. I was disappointed to find that there was no mention of grandparents in the index and very few in the book itself.

Another important relationship which is not much mentioned in the literature is that between the maternal and paternal grandparents. For me this has been one of the great discoveries of becoming a grandmother. The Jewish culture has a word for this most important relationship, describing as *makatonim* the people who are the in-laws of one's adult children. The 'other' grandmother can be a marvellous friend, confidante and ally, or a cause of anxiety, jealousy and irritation. Some grannies hardly meet, or are kept apart by geographical distance or by their adult children. But since I am extremely fortunate in my *makatonim* I know that this is a relationship which can lead to friendship of a very special sort.

DIFFERENT STYLES OF GRANDPARENTING

There are many different ways of being a grandmother. One American study listed five different styles of grandparenting:

'Formal' where lines between parenting and grandparenting are clearly demarcated,
'Fun–seekers' who are characterised by informality and playfulness,
'Distant figures' who see their grandchildren infrequently,
'Surrogate parents' who assume real responsibility for the child, and
'Reservoir of family wisdom' in which special skills and knowledge are dispensed.[21]

However, reality is more complicated and most grandmothers adopt a mix of styles to suit themselves, their grandchildren and the occasion. Recent research has shown that what a grandmother actually does depends on the age of the child, on the marital status of the parents, on social class, education, income and on her own personal inclinations.[22]

I have to admit that for me the 'fun-seeker' role is usually predominant. I love to build sand castles on the beach, to play hide and seek, to put on some music and have a dance, to read aloud or play a game of cards. On the other hand, there are times when being a 'surrogate parent' seems the most important role of all, reflecting my principle that the first responsibility of a grandmother is to support the parents. Being a surrogate parent may run from caring for a child on a regular day each week or giving parents an occasional child-free weekend to taking on the long term role of the parents, if they are not able to look after the children themselves.

The idea of the grandmother as a 'reservoir of family wisdom' raises the issue of the place of grandmothers in the transmission of culture. Being a 'reservoir of family wisdom' is not very satisfying if that wisdom is not valued and wanted. For many grandmothers the hardest part of the job is accepting that things have changed and that their priorities are not those of their children and grandchildren. Does it matter, they ask themselves, if the baby is up all evening and half the night, if the toddler is still not potty trained, if the child dictates the family menus, if the classics of children's literature are only known as Disney movies, if the teenager never listens to classical music?

However, perhaps grandmothers should not get too hung up on the details of child-rearing? If the baby is up all evening, that may be because the parents really want to spend time with him or her, having been out at work all day, and the baby wants to spend time with the parents. If the children's favourite foods are included in family meals, that may reflect a wider respect for the individual child and his or her own choices. In other words, does it matter if some parts of the package are not as they were thirty years ago, if the package is basically a good one and the children are happy and thriving?

A TWO-WAY TRANSMISSION OF CULTURE

The part which grandmothers play in the transmission of culture is complex and takes us to the heart of what it means to be a grandmother. Most grandmothers assume that they will teach the songs and poems which they learnt as children, will pass on family stories and rituals, will help the child to practice skills such as cooking, sewing, music making and so on. One of my few memories of my paternal grandmother, who died when I was five, is of her teaching me to kneel by my bed to say my prayers.

As the world changes some aspects of culture seem to pass down the generations more easily. I have found that I can bring pleasure to my grandchildren and enliven dull journeys by being able to recite Hilaire Belloc's poem about Jim, who was eaten by a lion, or the one by T.S.Eliot about Skimbleshanks, the cat of the railway train. On the other hand, some of the books which I loved most as a child seem unreadable today.

The transmission of culture is not a one-way process. As they grow, grandchildren enrich the lives of their grandparents in many different ways, of which being kept in touch with the changing shape of culture is just one. The grandchildren's enthusiasms may range from the toddler's Teletubbies to the teenager's concern for human rights or the environment, for music or art, or film or clothes. Currently I am being educated about Pokemon cards, which despite their arcane rules clearly involve a great deal of satisfying social interaction. I am learning that the novels of Jacqueline Wilson are much more relevant to the lives of children today than the tales of bravery in distant parts of the British Empire which I loved as a child. And I can see that the Harry Potter books are on their way to becoming the classics which our grandchildren will read to their grandchildren.

At one level it is fun to be kept in touch with all these developments. At a more serious level, one might argue that the ways in which ideas travel between grandmothers and grandchildren make this relationship one of the highways along which culture is created, maintained and transformed. To be a grandmother is to be linked with time past and time to come - which is what I was trying to say in the following poem:

POEM FOR MY GREAT-GRAND-DAUGHTER

When first the drama rolled, I was the star,
But knew it not, nor knew my mother's part.
Did someone telephone the new grandma,
As I lay wrapped in dead great granny's shawl?

Next time I played the mother. Full of joy,
Self-doubt and pride, I showed my daughter off.
Burden and bliss together seemed to melt,
In a new sense of what my mother felt.

When next the drama rolled, I was grandma,
Recipient of the phone call, rushing
To greet my daughter's daughter, the new star,
To tell the first great grandma she was on.

The years, our lives, the parts we play revolve.
Each time we understand the drama more.
But now there is a question in my heart -
Will I be there to play great-grandma's part?

GENERATION TO GENERATION

Joan Bakewell

My first grandchild was born as my father lay dying. The old man, his white hair lolling on the pillow, would enquire huskily, "Is the baby born yet?" He was waiting. At the other end of the country a young couple, in the full bloom of health and scarcely a year married were waiting too. Still further away, in Aberdeen, I was busily going about my business, making a television programme charting the fate of a whistle-blower penalised for his conscience. The producer and crew were well aware I was expecting an important family phone call. It came at 10.30 at night, at which point we adjourned for drinks to the hotel bar. The next morning I flew to Heathrow and drove directly to the cottage hospital where a room was already filling up with flowers. My father went on waiting.

A week later the new family drove north. With infinite tenderness my son lifted his newborn into the lap of his dying grandfather. A bubble of saliva, glistening and pure, hovered on the baby's full lip. Above him, my father's face, sagged with age and illness, took on sudden energy. He had lost the power of speech by now but his entire body was galvanized into response. He roused himself as far as he could, rocked the small bundle where it lay and made noises we could clearly

Joan Bakewell has been a broadcaster and journalist since the mid-nineteen-sixties. Over the years her best-known TV programmes have perhaps been Late Night Line Up *and* The Heart of the Matter. *She is now Chair of the* British Film Institute. *She has two children and six grandchildren.*

interpret as of welcome and delight. The effort was huge. In the intensity of the moment I know I was smiling a huge smile of happiness at something completed. My son smiled back. There was nothing to say. Two days later my father died. And a new life, my grandson's, had entered my own.

Now I have a small harvest of grandchildren. On each arrival there is a rush for overnight bags and travel. Several times I have been met at airports flying in from my own career to the heart of family life. Grannies often have paid jobs these days, no longer boiling kettles in the kitchen as they used to do in old films. And that engagement with the larger world keeps the new generation of grannies in touch with what will be commonplace in their grandchildren's lives. On the occasion of one grandchild's arrival I flew in from reporting in Florida on threats to abortion clinics from the religious right. The campaigners used their own children to propagandize their case. Each child was kitted out in a T-shirt that read, 'I am a survivor of the other holocaust'. I was appalled not only by the outrageous logic but by the calculated manipulation of children. What kind of world would my grandchildren be growing up in?

THE IMPORTANCE OF LIFECYCLE

Being a grandparent comes as a delightful surprise no one tells you about. The feminist generation, coming to adulthood in the 60's, who have so consistently mined their own lives for copy - relationships, parenting, the menopause, the glass ceiling, divorce, the empty nest – have yet to reach this later stage. So grandparenthood has not yet been examined for its full significance in the lifecycle of women and their place in society. When it is - and perhaps these essays are a start - the status of the old and their place in the changing patterns of family life will begin to get the attention it deserves. For these years need not be dominated by depressing and problematic issues. They are full of unappreciated rewards. Something to look forward to as the magazine-fuelled efforts to stay fit, stay young, give way to quiet resignation that time will have its way with all of us.

The fact is that grandparents enjoy the luxury of indulging two nostalgias: reliving the memories of their own childhood, and reliving the memories of when their own children were small. So there is much to wallow in. I have hoarded letters, photographs, diaries and school records from my earliest days. My grandchildren will not be writing letters, they'll be sending e-mails. So these simple relics themselves show how different my life already is from theirs. That's the story all grandparents have to tell: the story of the recent past or what my grandchildren call 'the olden days'. If you can remember as far back as the war that's a bonus. Bombs on London! Only one egg each a week! Tales of a household without telephone, washing machine or dishwasher hold them spellbound. The idea of there being no television amazes them. If this all begins to sound like the Monty Python sketch about living in a shoe-box on the M1, well, they haven't heard of Monty Python either. For a brief space of time what you know is magical and strange to them. They lap it up and you, for a span the keeper of the world's collective wisdom, can pass onto them a sense of changing times and customs that lays the foundations for a later and more mature sense of history.

The crux is, of course, just how much things have changed since your children's childhood; since your own. Now there are disposable nappies and velcro, Calpol and immunisation, buggies and wetwipes. Then there was discipline, respect, Sunday School and syrup of figs. But what's important is not that one set of values has taken over from another, but that with grandparents alive and active for so much longer, different sets of values co-exist and influence each other.

For example I am troubled that families now seem so totally child-centred. The needs, desires, demands of the child seem to dominate the domestic agenda. The needs and concerns of the parents - the man and woman whose loving commitment created these children – somehow have to wait. In many families children decide for themselves when they go to bed, decide what they want to eat, where they want to sleep. And if it is with their parents in their bed, so be it. It's only a phase. But what is not a phase is the practise of conceding at every turn to the demands of the child. This is surely flawed training for the real world where we all have to live with, and accommodate with good grace, the priorities of others.

At the same time I am impressed by the patience shown by young parents keen to understand rather than dominate their children, and their forbearance in the face of provocation. Where my mother would have unhesitatingly slapped me, and I would have lost my temper, I watch time and trouble being taken to help a child to the appropriate behaviour. It seems to me that this kind of parenting, ever more common in the present generation, is nothing short of heroic.

With so many changes from one generation to the next, there are bound to be tensions. The temptation to interfere with helpful advice, and the urge to insist that it is taken, comes easily to women who've forged their own lives in the face of a recalcitrant system. So the acceptance that your own children's generation is now in control doesn't come readily. There have been times when my eager suggestion that, "In my day we did it this way," has elicited a gentle but purposeful response, "Yes, but that was then, and this is now."

A TIME TO ENJOY

On the other hand, defeat being inevitable, it is better to concede with a good grace. And there is a certain satisfaction in the knowledge that this is indeed now, and that grandchildren are not our responsibility. In society's terms I have fulfilled my obligations, putting my energy, my commitment and my ideas into bringing up my children. Now I can enjoy the pleasures of grandchildren without having to agonize over matters of discipline, schooling, bedtimes, and television-watching. I feel I've earned my place as the matriarch who is found an armchair by the fire, and simply enjoyed as the bringer of extravagant and unexpected treats. Treats that turn out to give me as much pleasure as them. It is a time to enjoy and reap the benefits of earlier efforts.

And blessed are the grandparents whose children haven't taken up a posting in Dubai or decided on a career in the Australian outback. My generation can't expect as easy and regular access to grandchildren as was once the case. We have to work for it, and be able to afford the trips. On the other hand there is now e-mail and if there's a case for persuading the over-sixties to get on-line it is the prospect of staying easily in touch. Grandchildren are, of course, ahead of that particular game.

So what does being a grandparent teach you? I arrived at the role with fairly fixed notions derived from 30 years earlier about how families can and want to live. I've modified those views now in face of the evidence. My grandchildren enjoy the benefits of having full-time mothers at home and I see quite clearly how much their constant engagement from minute to minute reinforces the whole nature of the family unit and the children's sense that they are the heart of it. I didn't do it that way. I took the freelance route of dipping in and out of the world of work, depending on a procession of au pairs to smooth the transition. It wasn't entirely satisfactory. But then no system meets entirely the need of each person involved.

From the vantage point of age, I can see that this remains the great dilemma of our society – how to bring up children to their maximum benefit, while at the same time meeting the needs and rising expectations of working women. My generation didn't expect much, and so were delighted to get a little opportunity here and there. This isn't the case now. Women feel wronged and resentful if their career chances don't exactly match those of men. It remains the great unresolved issue of our times, not much nearer a solution now than it was when my own children were small. Perhaps my tales of how it used to be - how my teachers had to leave their jobs when they got married in order to look after their husbands, how using baby-sitters and nannies was seen as a cop-out - may console those women burning with ambition to be both a career star and a doting mother.

These, I know, are the golden days, while my grandchildren are small. The time is not long now before we reach the tough teenage years when grandparents will definitely not be part of the scene. I can expect to see them less often as visits to the dinosaurs at the Natural History Museum give way to clubs and discos, shopping and back-packing. But perhaps even then, when parents are being oh, so difficult, I might offer an alternative voice, and elderly subversive support. Yet still, and for the far future, I harbour the hope that one dying day, someone will feel it worth travelling to where I am, to lower a tiny bundle into my withered arms as one generation again gives way to the next.

NEWER RECRUITS

GOING DOWN MY NAN'S

Shena Mackay

JUGGLING WITH TIME

We grannies live in contradictory times: in the sad laddish world of the television comedian it's business as usual as far as ageism and misogyny are concerned; meanwhile politicians have woken up to the usefulness of grandparents in child-care but the government has raised the retirement age, and advertisers are torn between employing granny stereotypes, from the easily-shocked octagenarian (as if grannies haven't a lifetime's experience) to the roller-blading harridan, and courting the 'grey pound'.

Of course not all grandparents are grey; they never have been - my own mother, as a fairly youthful granny, was irritated by depictions of grannies dressed in bonnets, shawls and button boots, fashions more appropriate to the times of her own great grandmother. So perhaps nothing has changed much; societies have always shown ambivalence towards and a tendency to stereotype the granny figure, who appears variously as matriarch or monster, wise woman, fairy godmother or wicked witch, tragic pensioner or even the little old lady in lavender and lace that Gracie Fields sang about.

Shena Mackay has been writing for over forty years, starting in her teens. Her novels include Redhill Rococo, *winner of the* Fawcett Society Prize, *and* The Orchard on Fire, *shortlisted for the* Booker, Saltire and McVitie's *Prizes. She has three daughters, two grandchildren and lives in south London.*

Most of the time, though, grandparents are simply too busy to pay much attention to foolishness and sociological and anthropological questions. Recently one of my friends remarked, "I'd no idea being a grandmother was such hard work." She has a demanding job and often drives a long distance to look after her daughter's very young children when their parents are working and there's no other child-care available. My friend, a 'single granny' like me, loves spending time with her grandchildren but it's true to say that her daughter couldn't manage without her; here as often, grandparenting is an extension of parenting and she's doing it for her daughter as much as for the children.

Much as she adores her grandchildren, she admits privately to feeling trapped in her new role: "I feel I still have a career to 'do' - places to see - on my own, for me! They don't always fit in with being a grandmother." That said, the grandparent/ grandchild tie is a symbiotic one. I'll never forget how my children cheered up my mother when she was ill, simply by being themselves, plonking a cat or a picture book on her bed, demanding a story, and it was she who taught them all to read.

Time, the traditional attribute of the grandparent, is not always easily found and the harrassed grandmother can find herself juggling hers as frantically as she ever did, among work, children, grandchildren and elderly relatives. One of my grandchildren's grandfathers has retired recently but most of the grandparents I know are still working, and I imagine that those of us who are self-employed will be working until the day we die, unless rescued by some economic miracle such as an unexpected pension, the sale of film rights to Hollywood or a lottery win. I earn my living by writing, which means there is always some project on the go or looming on the horizon, whether it is a book review, an article, a short story or novel, and I worry sometimes about meeting deadlines so that I can be available when needed.

My work also includes some travelling, in this country and abroad, and this can lead to real dilemmas. For example, when the news came that my daughter Rebecca was expecting her first baby I had a long-standing agreement to go to New Zealand for a couple of weeks, an exciting and important trip which involved many people and much organisation. But the baby was due two weeks before my departure. At once New Zealand became the lesser event.

We arranged that I would stay with my daughter and son-in-law immediately the baby was born so that I could help out and, of course, be with my first grandchild. But, again, the baby was late, and as the days passed I was agonising over cancelling New Zealand at enormous inconvenience and financial cost to others, because, although the family said I should honour the agreement, there was no way I was going to be in the Antipodes while my daughter gave birth. Harry saved the day by arriving safely before I had to leave, so I did spend a little time with him, and Becky's sister came to stay with the new parents, which meant I didn't mind leaving quite so much.

JOINING THE CLUB

I have three daughters and two grandchildren and two more on the way. One of my sisters is a granny and several friends became grandmothers at about the same time as I did, joining a club whose members can exchange stories about the delights of this stage in our lives without risking charges of being boring or smug, as well as our anxieties about these little hostages to fortune. For us Miranda's 'brave new world, that has such people in't' is also Huxley's *Brave New World*. We don't stop fretting about our own children, however grown-up and successful they might be, and now we wonder how our grandchildren and their children's children will fare in a future of unimaginable, to us, scientific and technological developments; will our descendants be clones of themselves or have the benefits and drawbacks of eternal youth? For the present, outbreaks of meningitis make our blood run cold and we worry about pesticides in food and genetic engineering of crops, as well as world-wide religious fundamentalism. Also, the pleasure and privilege of having grandchildren brings sympathy for the distress of grandparents denied access to their grandchildren, and vice versa, and support for any projected legislation to ensure grandparents' rights.

Perhaps you have grown a bit of a carapace over the years; grandchildren make you as vulnerable again, as heartbroken by suffering and the fragility of all children, as you were when you held your own babies in your arms. As far as you're concerned the polar icecap can stop melting right now, endangered animals and plants must survive, nuclear non-proliferation treaties should be signed immediately and all third-world debt written off forthwith. Grandchildren won't allow your conscience to rest. You don't have to visit a refugee camp, as I did a few years ago when one daughter and her husband were working for an NGO, to be aware of the gross unfairness of the world: all you have to do is transpose images of your own grandchildren onto the faces in those television scenes of war and famine. Looking at my grandchildren and thinking about those to come brings to mind Laurence Binyon's poem:

> O World, be nobler, for her sake!
> If she but knew thee what thou art,
> What wrongs are borne, what deeds are done
> In thee, beneath thy daily sun,
> Know'st thou not that her tender heart
> For pain and very shame would break?
> O World, be nobler, for her sake!

I was fifty when I joined the grandparents' club and I've been just wild about Harry for five years now and half-crazy for the love of Daisy for three. I have known them both since they were a few hours old. As far as I'm concerned, being a granny means having child art on my walls again and more photographs than frames and albums to put them in, and treasured blurred black and white photocopies of print-outs

from ante-natal scans. I go home from visits with wilting
presents of flowers and leaves in my bag and peel-off stickers
on my clothes and I'm tempted by mail-order catalogues of
children's clothes. Like other grandparents I know, I'm torn
between spoiling them and spoiling their appreciation of
presents by giving them too much; many children nowadays
have so many toys and outings that we worry that they won't
get as much pleasure from them as we, who had fewer, did.

My heart melts at the children's metaphysical questions and
funny or poetic sayings and again as I watch my grandson
charging round the playground in a gang of little boys
shouting, "I am an alien from out *of* space," or being a king,
solemn and regal in green satin and a golden cardboard crown,
in his first nativity play, or my toddler grand-daughter
demonstrating how high she can jump, with both feet firmly on
the floor: later I couldn't care less if she's the best or worse in
the ballet class; for me she'll always be the prima ballerina.
I've learned to love Pingu - one of my prized ornaments is a
Pingu made from the inside of a kitchen roll - and Thomas the
Tank Engine, Percy the Park Keeper, Bob the Builder,
Spiderman, Superman, Luke Skywalker, Buzz Lightyear et al.

Even so, many cynically-marketed toys are depressingly
ugly. I hope that these clunky plastic characters won't be the
only heroes the children, born into a tarnished and
disillusioned climate, will ever know.

THE LINEAGE

If having grandchildren means falling in love all over again
and reinforces your engagement with the world, it also brings
a sense of continuity. When our children were growing up my
former husband and I had no video camera but we can relive
moments from their childhoods and catch glimpses of our
children in these new little people, so like our children in some
ways but coming with a different set of genes and family
history that makes the unfolding of their personalities so

interesting. The importance of continuity is demonstrated by the acknowledgement in recent years that we all have a fundamental emotional as well as biological need to know who we are. But perhaps the fact that many people, as they grow older, develop a belated interest in their ancestry shows that the roots of the family tree, stretching into the future as well as the past, can be a consolation for our own mortality.

Writing this, I find myself drifting off into memories of my own grandmother and my mother as a granny. How I wish that they could see my grandchildren, and hope that somehow they can. Yesterday I visited their great grandfather with my grandchildren; today I came across the pair of tiny blue socks that my grandmother knitted for one of my babies, which I have kept for more than thirty years. The poem I quoted above comes from a copy of *The Oxford Book of English Verse* with a time-speckled fly-leaf bearing my great grandfather's signature, dated 1906.

Three-year old Daisy has become intrigued by family relationships, asking questions about my mummy and granny, where they live and if they have the same faces as I do, and eyes like hers. She knows that her middle name, Morag, was her great-granny's name. It's fascinating to watch her mentally navigating her expanding universe, collecting information and establishing her place in the scheme of things. On a recent trip to an animal sanctuary she remarked wonderingly, "I didn't know there were any owls in my life!"

"I'm going up my Nan's after school." When I started school in Canterbury at the age of five I didn't know what other children meant when they said that. Sometimes they went *down* their Nans' houses. For some reason I pictured a lane, an overgrown cabbagey garden and a rabbit hutch. I had a beloved Granny who lived in Scotland, so when I understood what a nan was, I envied those children going up and down their Nans'. A Nanny, as Nans were sometimes called, was not to be confused with the equally mysterious figure of the capped and aproned Nanny in books such as 'Now We are Six'.

Encountered at a children's party, a Nan was a formidable figure in a flowered overall who plonked a mound of blancmange on your plate while you sat quivering with the jelly, too tongue-tied to say you didn't like it. She was an invaluable second line of defence, as in, "I'm telling my Nan, so there!" and even, "My Nan's coming up the school about you!", and she knitted pixie hoods, balaclavas and mittens that were threaded through the coat sleeves on elastic, and provided Rupert Annuals and big birthday cards with glittery numerals.

Notwithstanding, to actually live with your Nan seemed sad; there were a brother and sister at our school who did, and they looked like a little old nan and grand-dad themselves. If, God forbid, anything happened to my grandchildren's parents, I would feel it my duty, as well as my strongest desire, to look after them. In negotiation, naturally, with their other grandparents. As it is, my dream is that, when circumstances allow, some of them at least will be able to come up or down my house after school, and that someday I'll have a house big enough for them all to come to stay.

My grandchildren live in Southampton and I live in London. I see them at least once a fortnight. Sometimes they drive up, very often I take the train from Waterloo. The journey usually takes over two and a half hours each way. I liked playing with my own children and I'm quite happy to get down on the floor with the Lego and trains or to be a giant, policeman, burglar, dragon, or whatever is required. There's nothing like observing woodlice and snails, making castles in a sandpit or watching bubbles drift over the garden to make your own problems float away. Symbiosis again. Sometimes I give my daughter a break, at others I enjoy her and my son-in-law's company.

It's said that mothers of daughters have a stronger bond with their grandchildren than the mothers of sons, even a slightly stronger claim on them, (wasn't it Robin Hall and Jimmie McGregor who sang, "Ye cannae push your granny off a bus... Ye cannae push your Granny, cos she's your mammy's mammy... You can push your other granny, cos she's your daddy's mammy..."?) That's nonsense of course, and one can't generalise. Geography and all sorts of factors play their part. All I know is that I'm very fortunate in being close to all my daughters and my sons-in-law, and that I agree with other maternal grandmothers that it's worse when your daughters give birth than going through it yourself.

A CHANGING ROLE?

With reference, though, to grannies being pushed off buses, being a grandmother can bring a sense of empowerment at a time when women often complain of having become 'invisible', when they are overlooked in shops and shoved aside at bus stops for example. Not long ago I added my voice to that of a woman who remonstrated with a mother who was viciously smacking her child at a bus stop. The smacker shouted, "You don't know what you're talking about!" I heard myself replying, "I'm a mother and a grandmother, and I *do* know what I'm talking about."

   I come from a matrilineal tradition of grandmothers. I scarcely remember my father's parents who died when I was very young. My maternal grandparents were enormously important to me, as my mother was to her grandchildren. They were educators, arbiters of taste, and of morality, with high standards, as well as being fun. My life is very different from my granny's; Mary Carmichael was married to a Presbyterian minister and had the duties and social position of a clergyman's wife. I am divorced and make my living as a writer. Granny lived all her life in Sotland, the land of her birth, apart from visits to her children; now most of my family is in England.

   However, there are times when I'm very conscious of her legacy, songs and poems that she loved, for example, that move me, and I can appreciate that it must have been painful for her when all her children were so far away. Her son made his life first in Argentina and then Italy, her elder daughter and her doctor husband went to Newfoundland and Canada, where their children grew up, and my parents moved south to England. I feel for her now when I miss my own children. My youngest daughter lives in New York and my eldest daughter and her husband, presently in Aberdeen, worked abroad for some years, in dangerous situations, and probably will again, but that is something I don't want to think about. At the moment I'm just looking forward to their first baby. Three of my sister's grandchildren are in Australia, so that it's hard for her to see them comparatively infrequently and miss out on the day-to-day business of their growing up. The global village is all very well; I prefer an imaginary village, Utopia-on-Sea, where the whole family is within walking distance of each other.

My mother had eleven grandchildren and lived to see three of her great-grandchildren. She was the only grandparent my children knew, (they have got to know their grandfather, my father, in adulthood) after their great-granny died when they were very small. Their father was orphaned at an early age but two of his aunts played a grandmotherly part in their lives; one in particular, Aunt Diana, a woman of great courage and resource, then in her forties with a full-time job and various voluntary commitments, had taken on four teenagers when she brought my husband and his brother and sisters from India to London, selling her flat to buy a house to accommodate them.

My sisters and I grew up feeling that we were a small family; we enjoyed wonderful holidays with our grandparents but we hardly ever saw our few cousins. Now we're all part of a vast extended family which is fairly typical of many at the beginning of the twenty-first century in that we've had our share of sorrow, estrangements, divorce and remarriage. Do we, I wonder, see our roles as Grannies, in a so-called post-Feminist and rapidly-changing world, as essentially different from those of our predecessors? Only, I believe, in practical rather than emotional ways. We want to hand on our heritage from our own grandmother, and them to love and respect us as we did her. At my mother's funeral it was touching to hear several of her grandchildren give their accounts of her and to hear what had meant most to them as individuals.

Among my grandchildren's story books are some in the *Katie Morag* series by Mairi Hedderwick. I think particularly of *Katie Morag and the Two Grandmothers*. Grannie Island farms on a Scottish island, drives a tractor and wears wellies, while Granma Mainland is an urban sophisticate in high heels. Both Grannie Island and Granma Mainland, with their peculiar qualities and values, enrich Katie Morag's experience and teach her important things. At times I feel like Grannie Island, while Val, the children's Nanny, is Granma Mainland but we can change identities. In other words, the role of the grandmother is flexible and variable, and there is as much pleasure in learning from and about your grandchildren as there is in teaching them.

GRANDMA: MARK 2000

Claire Rayner

THE IMAGE

If I had been asked back in the nineteen-thirties what grandmothers were for, I would have had no hesitation in saying that they were for mothers to hate and argue with, and to tell you off for telling things to that were none of their bloody business.

That, after all, was my personal experience of the only grandmother I had to observe. The other one (and it was many years before I discovered there had actually been another) had died long before my birth.

This is perhaps an obvious way in which to make the point that individual experience varies vastly. That which is an obvious truth for one person will be anathema to another. That being so - and if people think about it they must surely admit to its truth - how is it that a stereotype of *The Grandmother* has been able to develop? Did so many people have apple-cheeked white-haired darlings wearing black bombazine over their ample laps and full of wise saws and sweet stories inhabiting their chimney corners? Did so many people actually grow up in houses that had chimney corners, come to that?

Claire Rayner has been an agony aunt and advisor on personal, health and family issues for nearly forty years. Using several pseudonyms as well as her own name, she has published dozens of practical guides to living and also works of fiction. She has three children, two grandchildren and lives in Harrow.

Yet there sits the stereotype, glorified in children's storybooks, in greetings cards, in advertising, in knitting patterns, everywhere. Where does she come from? Is she the imaginative artefact of millions of lonely or unhappy children, invented as a figure to love and trust instead of the disappointing parents or carers of reality? Or was she invented by just a couple of story-tellers with wider than average influence and foisted on the rest of us to our disadvantage?

The answer actually matters less than the fact of the disadvantages conferred by the existence of the stereotype. Because of Madam Applecheeks there are bitterly disappointed children and, equally importantly, disappointed young parents everywhere.

As an agony aunt, I lost count of the letters I had from young mothers complaining with considerable bitterness of the 'meanness' and 'selfishness' of their mothers/mothers-in-law who were not particularly interested in their children, who wouldn't baby-sit if they could possibly get out of it, who only gave niggardly presents and generally whooped it up living their own lives instead of being what 'grandmas ought to be'.

I have to admit that I also lost count of the letters from grandmothers complaining with even more intense bitterness about the wickedness of daughters/daughters-in-law who refused them adequate access to their grandchildren, who never put them to bed at the right time/fed them properly/taught them decent manners and poisoned their little minds against their grannies.

It is indeed a protean relationship, one that is shaped by the many different pressures on it. The grandmother/ grandchild connection is, we must never forget, strongly mediated by the parents of the child as well as by the spouse of the grandmother. (If said spouse is the child's grandfather then maybe all will be easy but often in these days of mix and match marriages the grandmother's husband/lover is a complete outsider as far as the child is concerned. He may also, of course, have grandchildren of his own to whom he feels he owes an allegiance he does not owe to his partner's grandchildren. Complicated, isn't it?)

THE TRENDS

What other features of modern grandmother experience have appeared in the agony column mailbag over the past couple of decades? And I make no apology for using this source of information. At its height it delivered around a thousand letters a week, all filled not just with the minutiae of daily life but also the major issues. It may not be a statistical sample, in that it is doubly self-selected (first respondents elected to read my columns and then elected to write to me) but it is surely a big enough sample not to be negligible even if it isn't statistically perfect.

- Grandmothers are both younger and older than in previous decades. This is because there are two distinct trends. The women of the so-called Post Permissive era who became mothers at the age of sixteen or even younger and produced daughters who in their turn became mothers at the same age, make it possible for some grandmothers to be aged 32 or so; and the women who delayed motherhood into their late thirties and even forties for career reasons thus make their own mothers wait for grandchildren until aged sixty or even seventy plus.

- The concept of the housebound housewife with ample time and adequate energy to spare for domestic duties is vanishing. Always a middle-class phenomenon (most working class women have had to work outside the home to supplement family income ever since the Industrial Revolution) this woman now has a career of her own (a second one, or a return to an original one) or uses her time for personal gratification or for voluntary work.

- With the increase in disposable income among older people making them into 'Woopies', i.e. Well Off Older People, a phenomenon of the past decade or so, many grandparents see spending money as the best way to discharge responsibility to grandchildren. They may bestow lavish gifts, pay school fees, even set up Trust Funds. They prefer this to direct hands-on care of the baby-sitting sort. This means the relationship with the children may seem stronger to the grandmother who measures it in expenditure than to the children who measure it in time spent together.

- In some cases of extra-young parenthood the grandmother takes over the full care of the child. Thus a woman of, say, forty, still young and energetic enough to handle the demands of a small child (indeed still able to produce another infant herself if she chooses) may resolve her daughter's (in-law) difficulties as a young parent, possibly unsupported by the baby's father, by offering full-time care which lets the mother work or continue to live her own young life, even possibly attending school or college. The result is less a grandmother/grandchild relationship, more a foster-mother/child relationship.

- The frequency of family fracture among young people has led to many grandparents being cut out of the lives of grandchildren to whom they have bonded and who in their turn love their elders dearly. A divorced mother may remove her children from contact with paternal family, or use the children as weapons in a continuing battle between the parents; a disaffected daughter may behave similarly. Either way grandparents are, more and more, demanding 'grandparents' rights' in law, asking for legal changes to enable them to intervene in a grandchild's life after such parental break-ups. That this could add to the child's pressures and possible unhappiness seems in some cases of smaller importance than the rights of the angered elders.

THE REWARDS

All this is of course the gloomy side of modern grandmotherhood. For many of us - and here I get personal again, thinking of my grandsons (aged at the time of writing almost five and nine months respectively) - being a grandmother is all gravy.

I take a lot of pleasure in being with these small boys, keep a stock of books and playthings of all sorts at our home for their visits, have created rituals around cookie jars, the singing of special songs and computer games specially bought for them, which they love, and generally take great delight in the relationships. However, in both cases it is based strongly on the excellent relationships I enjoy (thank heavens!) with the boys' parents as well as with my own husband. In other words, my grandmotherliness depends heavily on the quality of my original mothering. And I suspect that is true for all grandmothers.

Or is that just another stereotype?

THE *NEW* GRANDMOTHER[23]

Claudine Attias-Donfut

A VISIT

Getting off the train at Rosporden station and walking along
the platform, I began to look eagerly for the escalator so as to
avoid lifting my heavy trolley suitcase. I had come to
Concarneau this particular week-end to visit my son,
Emmanuel, after just having returned from a long stay in New
York, during which time I had bought a number of presents
that were now in the suitcase.

The heaviest presents were the toys for Maxime,
Emmanuel's son, three years old and my only grandchild. I was
so occupied with trying to find the exit that I hadn't noticed a
little boy, only three metres away and gripping tightly onto his
mother's hand, who was jumping up and down, chuckling, and
waving his arms at me. It was Maxime, overwhelmed with joy
to see me getting off the train.

How he had changed since I had last seen him three months
before! He greeted me with such a flow of words that he
astonished me. I wasn't surprised so much by his stories of
train accidents which he had seen on the television since this

Claudine Attias-Donfut is Director of Research at the Caisse Nationale
d'Assurance Vieillesse *in Paris. She is the author and editor of a
number of books on intergenerational relations, and the co-author with
Martine Segalen of the first major study of grandparenting in France,*
Grands-Parents: la famille à travers les générations. *She has two sons
and one grandson.*

was a perfectly natural association with myself (whom he regularly saw coming and going by train), as by his ability to remember exact details about me. I am always very moved by the way he has attached himself to me and the fact that I am an important person in his world despite the distance that separates us (I live in Paris and he lives in Brittany) and the irregularity, from my point of view at least, with which we see each other.

Once he began to know how to speak, Maxime spontaneously gave me the name 'Madine', which was short for Mamy (*Grandma*) Claudine. Having been baptised by him I felt in some way that I had been re-born through my grandson. During the week-end I devoted myself totally to him and he, moreover, took it upon himself that I was 'his possession', and didn't like it at all if I did things not involving him. In this family environment where he is my only grandson, he tends to monopolise this grandmother who is devoted to him. He always wants me to be at his disposal, and I naturally oblige. We had to be like this given the space that separates us and the infrequency of our meetings. The less often we see each other, the more intense are the visits.

I always try to stay for several days so that I can be as near to him as possible. Holiday periods in summer or winter are the best periods when I can spend the most time with Maxime and watch him growing up. Things are more difficult when it is time to leave. I go away with a feeling of sadness, which he seems to share. Fortunately, the distance that separates us has not prevented us from building up a close relationship.

THE TRANSFORMATION

Maxime has changed my life. I think that he has been the biggest change to my life since my children were adolescents, at which time I revised not only my relationship with my own children, but also my idea of myself. When such changes occur they touch the very heart of how we relate to others, our relationship with work, and how we see ourselves. By being drawn into his small world, and becoming an important part of it, I have begun to step back from the active adult universe in which I had been enclosed since my children left home. It may seem a trifle banal to say that I am passing into a new phase of life. Nevertheless, this is what I feel.

Life changes often go by unnoticed and then suddenly take us by surprise. We don't see them coming because we are so busy with daily routines. When a grandchild arrives, we are caught up in other events of our personal lives and time passes us by. Which kind of events lead to others? In the precious moments when I can read to and play with Maxime there is a wonderful kind of symbiosis between us. Through his childhood I find that I am revisiting my son's childhood as well as my own. I become a child again for the third time, and there is a feeling of an elusive 'contemplation of eternity'. Maxime provides a window through which I can look at his imaginary and marvellous world of childhood, a world in which he is at his most alluring. This is why I have become a regular customer in toy, clothes and book shops for children. At the same time, having children and grandchildren is the best way to leave childhood and youth behind.

People who do not have children, and in a smaller way those without grandchildren, do not have the same experience of the passage of time and certainly have more difficulties in seeing themselves mature and age. This is because it is children and subsequently grandchildren who give us our place in our life course, and who help us to cross the temporal passages of our existence whilst at the same time bearing witness to the truth of our age. Children cannot be fooled. Even if they are unaware of their grandparents' wrinkles, their own existence is living proof of their age.

The arrival of a grandchild changes our relationship with time. It has the double effect of heightening our awareness of the process of ageing whilst at the same time bringing many gifts which lead to a more gentle acceptance of growing older.

Paradoxically, the presence of a grandchild can also lead to one feeling younger - through the identification with a young child and the feeling of renewal that this brings. This identification of the grandparent with the grandchild is one which many anthropologists have observed world-wide, and it is one that I too feel in the intimate relationship I have with my grandchild.

I also feel a change in my emotions. Problems encountered in my professional life seem to weigh less heavily and are brought into a new perspective. I am a little less available for my friends and other family members than I was before. But at the same time, family ties have become closer. When I took Maxime to visit my mother, who is disabled and who couldn't get out to visit him, it was as if I had brought her a present. It reminds me of a highly symbolic gesture that my son made once on Mother's Day when I was visiting him in Brittany. He had a bouquet of flowers, and in order to present them to me he had put them inside Maxime's carry cot and was holding both of them together, the flowers and Maxime. In fact, I feel the arrival of Maxime has been a great gift from my son, and I must acknowledge this by taking care of this grandson. At the same time I recognise that the gift he is offering me is in reciprocation for the mother that I have been to him and for having given him the gift of life and the desire to reproduce.

My role as a grandmother is more restrained than the previous role I had with regard to my children when they were small. Becoming a grandmother, of course, both prolongs and complements parenthood. But it is not a continuation of it, since the role of grandparent is very different. In so far as being a play-mate for my grandchild is concerned, I feel that I am much younger and that I am losing the seriousness that comes with parenthood, together with the austerity that I had previously attached to it. But it is not only what I do or say that is different. I am perceived in the eyes of little Maxime independently of my own behaviour. For him, things are perfectly clear and there is no confusion. He has his parents

and as far as he is concerned I am a completely different
person who is nevertheless important and interesting. He wants
to find out more about me, and whereas he has grown to
become my friend, and I can comfort him even in front of his
parents, he knows that I am not as central to his life as they
are. This is why separations are always quickly overcome,
even if they still retain a nostalgic feel about them.

NEW PRIORITIES

The arrival of this small child with its accompanying social
bond has completely changed and led to a redefinition of my
emotional life. I am the sort of person who gives much time
and importance to my work, as do most academics who do not
have - or no longer have - young children (and even some of
those who do). But the time I give to Maxime now holds a
greater priority for me than that of work. I plan week-ends and
holidays well in advance and stick to them at all costs. My
time is organised around these periods, as are my trips and
holidays.

To be sure, there are other things besides gratification.
Among the difficulties that I encounter in the role of
grandmother, the one that I feel the most is the sensation of
my limits, the physical fatigue at the end of several days with
Maxime which arises from carrying him in my arms, running
after him, and continually watching out for any potential
dangers (which seem to be more real for me now than they
were for my own children). Then there is that aspect of
wondering what I should or shouldn't do, new responsibilities,
and the uncertainties surrounding this new role.

How my life has changed since the arrival of Maxime! I
can still remember the day when I learnt the 'good news' from
my son's partner, who was already a mother with two children.
My relationship with these two children, a girl aged five and
a boy of ten, was one of friendship and outside of any notion
of kinship. From the moment I learnt that their mother would

bear the child of my son, and that these children would therefore become brother and sister to my future grandson, the relationship with them changed. The arrival of my grandson in a way sealed the alliance with this new family, with the mother as well as the children. My life was enriched not only by a grandson, but also through having a daughter-in-law and two beautiful step-grandchildren.

Maxime's birth happened a few months after I had started to work on a book about grandparents with Martine Segalen. We had already signed the contract with the publishers, Odile Jacob. I had therefore begun to work on, to read about, and to write about the subject of grandparenthood. My personal reference point concerning this subject was my maternal grandfather, who made a strong impression on my childhood and whom I loved and admired most. Like all the people that we interviewed in the survey for the book, young and old, I had a particular grandparent whom I idealised, this marvellous grandfather. It was the grand-daughter that I had been rather than the woman I have become that was the source of my thoughts on this subject.

My co-author, Martine Segalen, in contrast focused on her own grandchildren and also the role of her own mother toward her great-grandchildren. So her approach sprang from the grandmother that she had become. The arrival of Maxime, however, made me shift my views concerning how I approached this research on grandparenthood.

Before I knew that my daughter-in-law was expecting, the idea of being a grandmother was only a hypothetical possibility, a future which seemed to me to be little more than an abstract one. The child who didn't yet exist was unreal, reflecting the future and all the uncertainties that it holds. When I found out that this child was to be born, everything changed and reality made its mark. As the date of his birth approached, and preparations began to be made, questions arose over how his brother and sister would react, as well as over the new responsibilities of the parents, and of myself.

KNOWLEDGE AND EXPERIENCE

In what way has my research on grandparenthood influenced my own experience of this role? I can't really say for sure. Certainly it has made me think more about what it is to be a grandmother. Perhaps it has helped me to develop my relationship with Maxime and all the other important individuals in his life. But I can't be sure that my work has definitely had a strong impact on my experience of being a grandmother.

What I can say is that my research has not allowed me to steer clear of mistakes I make in the eyes of my son's household, even though I spent a lot of time analysing them in the book. They do, however, seem less dramatic and more easily and quickly rectified in a good-natured way than would have otherwise been the case. For example, like many other people whom we interviewed in our survey, I do not always agree with the way that my son is bringing up his child. I sometimes find that he is a little strict, and he finds me not to be strict enough. Instead of always respecting the rule of non-interference, which is the golden rule for grandparents and one which we have emphasised throughout our book, I have also tried different tactics or indirect ways (through books or talking) to convince him of the sound reasons on which my understanding of the right education of Maxime is based.

What he underlines, and is quick to make me understand, is the fact that he is the master in his home. The 'right distance', the sacrosanct right distance, is not always to be found instantaneously. It has to be sought by overstepping the mark sometimes, by getting too close and then withdrawing too far; and once attained this position has to be maintained with the utmost care. It is well known that theory cannot replace actual experience of relationships between individuals. What is certain is that being a grandmother altered the way that I worked on the book, and has changed my approach to the research concerning this aspect of family life.

By the time they had reached adolescence, my children had transformed my theoretical approach to the relationship between generations, one which was to be developed in my book *The Sociology of Generations*, published in 1988. Some of the analysis that appeared there can also be applied with modifications to grandparenthood. When confronted by their children becoming more and more autonomous, parents themselves enter a critical stage of their life. Their generation acquires a self-awareness through the challenges that their children present to them.

Only through a new generation can a true definition of the preceding generation be given, one which moreover is entirely consigned to the past. Through their children, parents receive this evolving image of themselves. Grandparenthood is the extension of this process. When these adolescents grow and become in turn parents themselves, the changeover is accomplished by a mutual redefinition of intergenerational relations as well as identities.

Drawing the line between being a parent and a grandparent is not straightforward. Many grandmothers have to fight against a compulsion to intervene. Perhaps this comes from an overlapping of roles, from a kind of lengthening and assimilation of their parental role into grandparenthood. But even so, the two roles should deal with very different situations.

Parents have the primary responsibility for bringing children up. That of grandparents is secondary - even though they are unique. The visit this week-end was a success because my being there had introduced an additional, festive dimension. I am Maxime's play-mate, and happy to be that. We have our shared games, plus reading and bed-time rituals. As I had been away for so long, he showed me all his new toys and other new things in the home. For example, in the garden he proudly showed me the new plants, trees and flowers, even if they weren't new. For Maxime, I am an outsider and a visitor who disrupts daily household routines as *well* as a full family member who plays a central part in family life. The duality is the essence.

I cherish these privileged moments with Maxime. I am fully aware that when he is older things won't be the same. Of course, I will try hard to maintain our friendship and to find things that we will have in common at all ages. But it is only during this period when he is small that we can create this bond of real friendship, a real couple of grandchild and grandmother.

THE *NEW* GRANDMOTHER

I sometimes have the impression that I am not representative of my generation, that of the sixties, since so much of my personal history seems to me to have been out of character with the collective period of history through which I have passed. Nevertheless, when I discuss these matters with other members of my generation, I do recognise that there are significant similarities in the importance that they attach to grandchildren, and in their relationship with them. Children behave and express attitudes with their grandparents that they wouldn't dare do with their parents.

I belong to the first generation which started to draw more widely on psychoanalytical methods in child-rearing. Grandmothers of my age are very concerned about their grandchildren and invest a great deal of time and energy. This is a personal experience, more individualistic perhaps than in the past. Even though I have the impression that my generation represents a turning point, with one foot in tradition and the other in more modern times, I also know that it is the fate of all generations to be only a transition between what has been and what is to become. My generation has lost a large part of the family and religious traditions that were still in place in our parents' time. Culture has altered radically.

As a result, I sometimes feel as though we now construct a kind of improvised handywork of tradition. We seek to compensate for the absence of inherited tradition by passing on a part of our selves, and through the quest for intellectual and emotional dialogue. The grandchild brings us sharply up against this chasm and the missing elements that are no longer passed from one generation to another.

My generation is at the age when our first grandchildren are just arriving or are still very young. The bond with this very young child is a kind of fusion and something to be marvelled at. Grandparents do not have a completely prescribed role, and we have seen in our research that there is a variety of styles of grandparenting. For myself, the mission of grandparents is to support parents in the education of their children. This is a role that they have always more or less played, and no doubt one that goes back to the mists of time.

What does change is our conception of education and the division of roles between parents and grandparents. Child-rearing styles are more tolerant, informal and orientated towards personal fulfilment for the child and the unfolding of personality. But difference in views between successive generations is inevitable, and requires constant adaptations between the three partners to this: grandparents, parents and grandchildren.

In spite of these transitions, and historical changes in style, some aspects of grandparenting seem irreducible. Grandparents have the psychological function of reassuring parents and grandchildren that they all have a place. They have the emotional task of opening up the family household to the outside world, and of being the mediators between its members. They have an important practical and supportive function through the helping hand and gifts that they bring. They have an intellectual function, through passing on interests, knowledge, and history. And finally, they have an existential role by being living proof of the reality and nature of kinship. Grandparents, as the symbol of family life itself, endow children with an identity, by enrolling them in the chain of generations.

MY FRIEND CATO[24]

Nell Dunn

MY GRANDMOTHER

Ever since I first remember seeing my maternal grandmother
I knew I was like her: that narrow face, those worried eyes.
When I was about seven she asked me who was the most
important person in the world to be friends with. She
eventually told me the answer was 'Yourself'. I loved being
with her and with my mother and my sister, all of us together,
this woman's world. Her name was Vera.

Once she took me to visit a cousin of hers who lay on a
sofa in a grand house: "I never sit, I always lie; it preserves a
woman's beauty." Ever since then I too have never sat, but
always lain. My grandmother wore soft tweed suits with capes
to match and embroidered satin nightdresses. I learnt later that
they were hand-me-downs from the cousin who always lay.
When I was quite a little girl, she told me to pinch the bridge
of my nose every morning when I woke up so I would have an
elegant narrow nose and not a boxer's snout. She also told me
not to frown as this would make 'cross' lines on my face.

When I went to stay with my grandmother, I slept with her
in the double bed with the giant coronet embroidered on the

Nell Dunn's best-known books are probably her novels Up the Junction
and Poor Cow, *and her best-known play* Steaming. *But she also has
written non-fiction, like* Talking to Grandmothers *from which the
passages making this chapter have been taken. She lives in London and
has three sons and two grandchildren. Cato is her first grandchild.*

white satin bed-head. We lay side by side under the white satin coverlet which also had a coronet to match. If I moved I woke her up, so I had to lie very still, and I longed for her to go to sleep so I could wriggle. It was on one of those visits that she told me her own mother had died when she was ten. She only heard about her death when her nanny came in in the morning and said,"Which dress will you wear today, Miss Vera?"

"My cherry dress please, Nanny."

"You can't wear your cherry dress today, Miss Vera, because your mother died in the night."

During the First World War she had driven an ambulance and been very dashing, so history relates. In the Second World War she worked for the Red Cross, packing cardboard boxes with food for prisoners of war. My mother took me and my sister to see her at work, and she paused for a while to show us the little bars of chocolate and the packets of ten cigarettes that went into each small cardboard box. She let us help pack them. She was already a widow, but she seemed happy in a room full of other busily occupied women. Later, after the war, she appeared pale and lost, and it seems sad that this generation of ladylike women were excluded from everyday employment and forced by their ladylike ways into the servitude of boredom.

Much later, when she was in a convent that looked after elderly people, I used to take my own children to see 'Great Gran' as she was called. We'd go out into the overgrown garden and sit on a bench while she fed the cats with morsels she had saved from her breakfast and told us stories about her Alsatian who had once followed a train she was travelling on, running along the track for nearly a hundred miles and meeting her at the other end. She told us about going to stay with her army brother in India, and riding side-saddle and hunting in Ireland, and once of having to work her passage home on an ocean liner to raise money in England because my grandfather had lost everything on the gambling tables and was being kept a prisoner at the Grand Hotel in Casablanca till he had paid the bill. I never knew if it was the Irish blood that invented these stories. Once when she was very, very old we took her for a walk and she fell in a stream. Her great-grandsons tried to pull her out, but she got the giggles and much to their glee flopped back in the muddy water.

Although I loved her and knew that in her own way and of her own time, she had been a good grandmother, I didn't want to be the same kind of grandmother. I wanted to know my grandson better from the beginning. I wanted us to be ordinary and everyday with each other. I wanted to be able to be cross with him and for him to be cross with me. I remember in Márquez' novel, *Love in the Time of Cholera*, somebody says, "By raising my children I got to know them and they got to know me and we became friends." In a milder sense this is what I hope for: that by helping to take care of my own little grandson, Cato, we shall become friends.

MY GRANDSON, CATO, AND HIS FAMILY

Roc, the eldest of my three sons, is Cato's father. Cassia is his mother; Nina is Cassia's mother and my co-grandmother. A home birth in Clerkenwell Green had been planned, but after Cassia had been eighteen hours in labour with Roc beside her and an excellent midwife attending, and Nina and I in the kitchen making food and drinks for everyone in a heat wave, it was decided that she was in too much pain and the baby wasn't making good progress. She was carried down the five flights of stairs into an ambulance and taken to hospital, with Nina and me following in the midwife's car.

EARLY DAYS WITH CATO

Cassia and Cato came home after only six hours in hospital, and Nina and I took it in turns for those first few days to shop and cook in the high-up Clerkenwell flat. "Don't expect any feelings, don't expect to be happy, just get on with being useful," I told myself, yet I felt quite lost. I wasn't the mother of the child. There was my eldest son with his eldest son, with new calls on his affection and new responsibilities. I thought, "Who does he think he is, this little intruder?" I had to get used to being a grandmother and not the little princess in the bed with the little prince - as I had been when his father was born. Instead, there I was with sleeves rolled up, being useful.

I felt big and clumsy beside this tiny creature who trusted me not to drown him, who half-opened his little shut eyes and uncomplainingly blinked at me, the clumsy grandmother in the apron, dredging up lost memories of how to hold him safely in the plastic bowl, my elbow crooked under his small skinny back, remembering to test the water with the inside of my wrist so that it wouldn't be too hot on his new-laid skin. All that tenderness, and yet I was adrift, speechless, uneasy with myself and new title, 'grandmother'.

As a mother I had been so in charge of my children; they were my little brood. We were here, we were there, and I became strong through bringing them up. They were very loyal and we were all together. What I found hard in becoming a grandmother was that I was much lower down the power scale. It was a humbling experience.

I knew that I had to make my own relationship with Cato with no one else there. It was a private matter between me and him. I didn't expect his birth to be such an enormous event in my life. Here I was, faced with a little baby who wasn't mine, and I saw I had to make a move to love without yet being loved. I came up against this icy, tight and calculating part of me: "Why should I give him anything? He's not mine." I did all the right things in the practical sense, but the love was slow in coming. Very slow.

Then one afternoon I'd taken him for a walk in the park nearby. He was about three months old and his mother was still breastfeeding him, so I couldn't go far. I was sitting on a bench in the rose garden when two Indian women came up with a little girl. They started admiring him and asked if they could hold him. It turned out they were mother, daughter and grand-daughter, and they were full of pleasure as they sat beside me on the bench, the sun glinting on their sparkling saris, and congratulating me on my immense good fortune at having a beautiful grandson. I felt very proud and then, as they handed him back, he smiled at me and I was suddenly, all at once, bowled over.

Overcome, I hid my face in his warm little stomach and I knew that, yes, I was immensely fortunate! And so it had begun, me and my friend Cato. During that autumn we got to know each other on our little adventures around his neighbourhood. . . .

CATO LEARNS TO GO DOWN STEPS

When I haven't seen Cato for a couple of weeks I am longing to see him, but I enjoy the longing, whereas I hated being apart from my own children. When they went to their father's for a week I found the separation very painful. I don't find this with Cato. I think about him a lot, but I don't need to live with him. One full day a fortnight is right for me at the moment. I do nothing else on that day but have a bath and breakfast, and then I go and fetch him. We spend the day together and at night I take him home.

I feel if I have him once a week instead of once a fortnight, I'm not going to be able to cope with my life. What about my life as a writer? I'm not sure if this fear is some endless, frantic struggle with time and an urgency that I've always had and should now let go of, or if there is some reality. I don't really know. Yet there are things that I couldn't do without him, like spending a weekday afternoon with friends and babies in the sun rather than being at home working. He takes away the guilt; if he's on my knee, I'm not idle.

I have to remind myself that he won't die if he gets bored or cross or cries. There's still a bit of me that thinks, "How disastrous!" Each time I have him I get more confident with him and he gets bolder. Last week I sat reading the paper while he crawled along the passage to the kitchen because May and Ivy were in there and he loves watching them. I had put a cushion at the bottom of the two steps going into the kitchen in case he fell and then I went on reading the paper in the sitting room. After about five minutes I heard this great shriek and ran out - he had tried to get down the steps and had got stuck halfway and panicked! He had not yet learned to turn around, so he had one hand on the step below and his other arm stuck desperately up in the air. He was howling with fright. I picked him up and he clung to me and I was touched that he could find comfort in me. He sat on my knee and sucked his fingers, and after a while he wriggled to get down and start on his adventures again. This time I came too and helped him turn round when he got to the steps so he went down feet first. He was pleased and went up and down several times. I clapped and he clapped too.

After lunch he fell asleep and I listened to the radio. When he woke we went to the bank on the number 11 bus to Sloane Square. We both got quite excited about our bus ride. We get on at a request stop and the bus comes over a humpbacked bridge, so you only see its red roof when it's nearly upon you. It was a struggle to hold Cato in my arms and fold the pushchair at the same time, and then flag down the speedy bus and leap, no hands, on to the platform, carrying baby and pushchair, and pretending it was easy-peasy, and I did it every day.

He loves kneeling up on the seat just inside the door and looking out. Usually I sit upstairs in the front of the bus, pavement-side, but it would have been tricky carrying him up the stairs, so now we've got a little routine of inside on the bench seat, him kneeling, nose pressed to the window, me beside him. I'm so proud when he goes out with me. I tell everyone he's my grandson. One day we'll sit on the top at the front and go all the way to St. Paul's Cathedral, me and my friend.

CATO IS NAUGHTY

Cato has caught on to being naughty. The first time I had to tell him off for taking unlit coal out of the fire. I put it back, saying, "No," and carried him to the other side of the room and gave him a toy to distract him. Directly I was looking away, back he crawled to the fire and took out the coal. I did the same thing again, but this time I watched him and, when he got to the fire and stretched out his hand, I said, "No" quite firmly. His hand stopped in mid-air and his back went quite stiff. After a moment his hand went out again rather tentatively towards the coal. "No!" I said, more strongly this time. His hand dropped and he began to howl, the loudest howl you ever heard. I picked him up and hugged him.

Later we were in the kitchen; I was making lunch and he was playing with the pots and pans. He navigated the two steps and crawled away towards the sitting room. A minute or two later I went to see what was going on and found he had filled the dogs' water jug with coal. "Cato!" I yelled and he looked apprehensively, so I showed him how to put the damp coals back, scooped him up and took him into the kitchen for lunch. . . .

In the afternoon, we go with Joy to visit Sharon and Wayne. . . . He falls asleep on the way back to my house and when he wakes up he doesn't want his high tea of baked beans on toast. I take him home to his mother. He is tired and cries in her arms. I am worried, but she says reassuringly, "Don't worry, it's the grannies; he always has too exciting a time when he goes out with the grannies and comes back exhausted." She takes off his socks and seeing his dirty little feet she says, "Cato, where did you get such dirty feet?" I slip quickly out of the door.

CATO GOES TO THE DROP-IN CENTRE

This morning, on the way back from fetching Cato, he and I go to a toy shop called Tiger Tiger and buy a farm. I remember all the excitement of buying toys for my son Jem, who could always coerce me into spending money. The farmhouse has roses growing up the wall and a red-tiled roof that you can lift off. There is an open-sided barn and a shed with three stalls. I would have liked one with a pond, but Jem isn't here, so my Puritan instinct gets the better of me and I choose the cheapest and a bag full of animals.

When we get home, we unpack the farm and arrange all the cows and horses and calves and pigs in place, including the girl throwing corn from a basket for the hens and ducks. We manage a few animal noises between us. I take Cato out into the garden and tidy up the geraniums since I plan to bring them indoors soon. The sun is shining and Cato crawls around the garden and I take his shoes off. It is such a beautiful hot September day, and soon it will be winter and too cold for such delights. . . .

He plays with the farm while I make him lunch of spaghetti and peas. After lunch I put him in the pushchair and we go out, heading south, through back streets, towards the river. In a little park in Fulham, surrounded by high flats and approached only by footpaths patrolled by tall mongrels with their noses perpetually to the ground on the look-out for fallen chips, is the Drop-In Centre. Here mothers and grandmothers and babyminders come each and every afternoon with their 'under-fives' to sit and chat and smoke a fag and drink a cup of tea, while Lorraine and Carly and Cheryl and Steven and Wayne and Jack and Cato play in the sand or on the train. We sit in the sun, this world of women, talking about how Clifford and Archie and Emma won't sleep in the afternoon, and always get a nappy rash after eating tomatoes. How Charlie never learnt to walk, but one day when he was eighteen months old he stood up and ran. . . .

After two hours I want to go home and I lift Cato up and carry him towards the pushchair. He starts to cry and I thought of my friend, Louise, and what she would have done. "Come and say 'Goodbye' to Cheryl and Victoria and Ellen, and then we are going home." I carried him around saying 'Goodbye', and he got into the swing and waved his hand enthusiastically, and then I said, "Now we are going home," this time he let me strap him in without protest. I must remember who is in charge, *me*, and then do things with style, including him and not just suddenly rush off! He fell asleep as I pushed him through the September afternoon sunshine.

When I have Cato on my own I am completely responsible for him and I feel much closer to him. When his parents are there I want to talk to them and tell them my news, and he wants to talk to them too, so sometimes we are rivals, and I retreat into the background and make tea and become a skivvy in the kitchen.

There is a sadness attached to being a grandmother. Is it because you are no longer in the very centre of life? There is a casting-off of power, you are not so absolutely essential as you were when you were a mother with young children. It is a shedding of responsibility, a movement towards death. Yet there is also a lightness, a freedom, and the sheer delight of having a child in your life again. I think of a grandmother, not in this book, saying to me, "I would like to be guardian to my grandchildren if anything ever happened to their parents. I sometimes wonder if I would be allowed to keep them, although I would fully understand if they wanted younger guardians. I have known them so well now that I feel I could continue and be loyal to what their parents would have liked. To me they are a continuation of my family. They fit, they belong. I feel so happy with those children."

HANDING ON

Amanda Goodfellow

How well I remember the telephone call which announced the safe arrival of our first (and so far only) grandchild, on New Year's Day, 1998. A surge of joy, of pure delight and anticipation swept through me, which surprised me by its strength. We had to give expression to it by whooping, throwing our arms into the air and dancing round the room, before toasting the newborn and his mother (our daughter-in-law) with champagne. Was it just the memory of my own four babies, and the pleasure they brought me, and the thought of being able to relive some of that pleasure again? Or an atavistic pride in having our name and genes passed on to a new generation, an affirmation of family continuity? A combination of both, I suspect. The emotion certainly felt primitive and unalloyed. It was definitely not connected however with the idea of myself as grandmother, newly promoted to the state of grandparenthood.

GENERATIONS PAST

My own grandparents had been remote and a little forbidding. My father's father was a much loved Manchester GP, who died

---

Amanda Goodfellow has been involved at various stages of her life in writing, publishing, running a smallholding and wholefood shop, health and social care research, therapeutic massage and complementary medicine. She has four children and one grandchild, and lives with her husband in Norfolk.

shortly after I was born. His wife, my paternal grandmother, was an eccentric widow when I knew her. She always dressed in old-fashioned black clothes, with long skirts, and wore a black straw hat both inside and outside the house. To us, she looked a little like a fairy-tale witch, especially as she had an aquiline nose and wrinkled brown skin. She was reputed in her youth to have chained herself to the railings outside Manchester Town Hall, in support of votes for women.

There were many family tales about her foibles, including one incident when she was said to have taken off her wig when playing bridge with friends and hung it on the back of her chair, because she felt too hot. I remember her as a somewhat anxious and severe figure of whom I was in awe, the two or three times that we stayed with her. The chief attraction of our visits was the box of marvellous mechanical and carved wooden toys, mostly dating from before the first world war, with which we were allowed to play as a special treat. They had belonged to my father and his two brothers and sister. Since Granny G. died when I was eight, and our visits to her were few, she impinged little upon my childhood world.

My maternal grandparents played a much greater part in my upbringing, since we lived with them all through the second world war, until my parents finally bought their own house near London in 1948. But they were not approachable people, and on the whole believed that children should be seen and not heard. My grandfather had been a high court judge in India, and was still an acting magistrate locally. He was very much the paterfamilias. The household was run for his convenience and comfort. Although we were constantly told how much he loved children, this was not evident to me. He chiefly delighted in feeding me bits of kipper on buttered toast from his breakfast, which he ate in solitary state after we had eaten ours. I thought this was an overrated activity.

My grandmother was a sad, frail woman, whom I loved, but in whose presence I didn't feel easy. Maybe this was to do with the fact that throughout my childhood expectations were

laid on me which I felt I could never quite match. It was as
though the reputations of my mother and my grandmother
depended upon my achievements and behaviour. She taught
me to play cards and cribbage, and encouraged my piano
playing. But I always felt that I was loved not for myself, but
for the successful person I might become.

Being sent to boarding school at the age of five heightened
my sense of loneliness and of being misunderstood by my
family. I remember that television was being introduced at this
time, and talked about in the press, though nobody I knew
possessed a set. In my boarding school in Berkshire, hundreds
of miles from my Devon home, I used to lie awake worrying
that this new invention would enable my mother and
grandmother to watch my every activity, and find me wanting.
This grandmother died of cancer when I was fourteen, after a
long period of sickness and suffering. My grandfather married
again shortly afterwards, and I saw very little of him
thenceforth.

What of my own and my husband's parents as grandparents?
Both sets were proud of their grandchildren, enjoyed their
company and gave generous and thoughtful presents. When my
first baby was born, in Cambridge, we were living only a half-
hour's drive from my parents' comfortable country home.
Although my mother was at a loss with small babies, she was
always happy to have me come and stay, feed me and cosset
me and give me a rest. She thus provided support and a
valuable resource, which I greatly appreciated and hope to
provide for my own children as they become parents.

Unfortunately we moved to Edinburgh shortly afterwards,
and I very much missed this contact when my three daughters
were born. My mother, and sometimes my father, would
occasionally come and visit us in Scotland, but we spent the
most time with them on our biennial trips south - at Christmas,
always celebrated at my parents' house, and over our regular
summer holidays in Norfolk. My own children remember them
with affection, but the two younger ones say they were a little

frightened of them. My parents were not warm, cuddly people, and our children found my mother's manner in particular rather strange. But they all loved going to stay in their old Essex farmhouse. My eldest daughter recalls the smell of toast burning on the Aga, my mother's cooking, and her terrier dogs. My mother used to come with the dogs to wake her up in the morning. There was a box of 'dog-chocs' which was kept as a treat for them, but which our children enjoyed eating surreptitiously. My father, like my grandfather, preferred to eat his breakfast on his own, in peace, so that he could read the newspapers, and was not pleased if interrupted by small children.

Of such small incidents are memories woven. Sadly, my parents both died while our children were still comparatively young. I am sure they would have come in to their own as grandparents when our children reached adolescence. My mother would have enjoyed visiting local stately homes with them, imparting her knowledge of antiques, and taking them, one at a time, to the theatre and ballet, as she had taken me when a child. And I think my father would have enjoyed teaching some of his skills, photography for instance, to our son.

My husband's parents, very different from mine, and much more demonstrative in their affection, lived in a small flat in London, but were always delighted to see us and to feed us copiously. Grandmother Ray, however, was a strict disciplinarian (partly because she thought she would be letting me down if she weren't) and could be quite fierce, causing some alarm among my permissively brought up children. Ray's idea of the child-rearing principles to which I adhered were more in her imagination than based on observation, and only applied when she was staying in our house, looking after the children on my behalf. When they stayed with her in London, there was unlimited television and trips to the excellent local ice-cream parlour. She and her husband too died only three years after my own parents. None of the four reached the age of seventy. This was a deprivation which I hope will not be visited on my grandchildren. I should very much like to see them grow up and to celebrate their majority at least, before I pass on. I want to be a part of their childhood lives and to be remembered by them for the good times we had together, and for the fun, and the learning. I would like them to feel that whatever happens to them, whatever they do, they will never lose my love. As long as I live, I shall always be there for my children and their children if they need me, a refuge and a reassurance.

MY OWN ROLE

I have a vision of my role as grandmother. When the grandchildren are born, I intend to make myself available in the traditional way, to help out as requested - even, if my daughters wish it, to be present at the birth. After my grandson was born, and my daughter-in-law had returned home, I stayed for ten days, did most of the cooking and looked after the baby at night so that she could get some rest. I gave advice when asked for it, but was also careful not to press my own views. With my own daughters I might be more assertive! Fortunately I get on well with my daughter-in-law, and don't recall any major differences of opinion.

As the babies grow, I shall teach their parents how to massage them, and encourage them to do so regularly. I look forward also to massaging my grandchildren myself from time to time. As a trained infant massage teacher, I don't often get to practice on real infants. We teach the massage strokes on dolls, leaving the babies to their own parents.

In the early years of my grandchildren's development, I consider my role chiefly to be one of support and encouragement. I would like my children and their partners to feel that they can come and stay with us whenever they feel like it, and make use of the space and facilities we can offer, which at present are considerably more than they can afford themselves. I should also be glad if they felt free to call for assistance to help them through a crisis, on the understanding that I have other commitments, and am not entirely at their beck and call. At this stage, I envisage the grandchildren coming with their parents, *en famille* - or with one parent, at any rate. I would enjoy doing with my grandchildren the things I did with my own children - reading to them, singing songs at bedtime, taking them for walks and expeditions and to the seaside, cooking good things to eat etc. - the stuff of a traditional domestic life.

As they grow, and become more independent, and secure in my company and my house, I would have them to stay and do more adventurous things with them, depending upon their interests and inclinations. At home, I would teach them some of my domestic skills, a number of which (such as darning socks!) are now almost obsolete. As a historian myself, who has made a particular study of the home life of women in past centuries, I would take particular pleasure in passing on some of this knowledge, in practical ways, to my grandchildren - thus giving them some understanding of where we have come from, and how much the world has changed, and is changing.

We could make bread together to bake in a brick oven, gather sloes and blackberries from the hedges to make wine and sloe gin, learn to recognize the herbs in my garden and what can be done with them, experiment with vegetable dyes, spinning and knitting. My grandson (unlike my own children) is already expressing a keen interest in gardening, which delights me. He can name all the flowers in his own garden already. So I certainly anticipate spending some happy hours with him in my garden, where he may, if he wishes, have his own plot to cultivate and grow pumpkins on which he can carve his initials. By making and doing things with them at home, I would hope to reinforce their sense of belonging to a family with history and traditions and stories to tell, and to promote their self-confidence, and their feelings of pride and security at being valued members of a lively clan.

Outside the home, there are many entertaining possibilities for time spent together. I would like to give my grandchildren experiences, not objects - my time and my attention doing things with them that they will remember with pleasure, and may open their eyes to new ideas and potential. I would like to be remembered for the fun we had together, not for the expensive presents given. I don't want to be seen as a walking cash machine in our too materialistic world, where children nowadays seem to be almost buried in toys of every kind from the moment of birth. But I expect I will give presents, of an educational nature. One of the best presents I ever received as a child was a beautiful German-made wooden recorder, which gave me hours of pleasure, and eventually led to my learning to play the clarinet.

I look forward to London sight-seeing excursions, visits to museums, theatre, cinema (especially the Imax cinema) and concert halls; river trips, days at the seaside in North-West Norfolk, where we used to take our own children, country walks and cycling picnics. I harbour an ambition to go ballooning, and would love grandchildren to share the experience. Certainly we shall go on the London Eye, though I'm not sure about the Millennium Dome.

COMBINING WORK AND GRANDPARENTING

But at the same time, although I can see myself doing all these things, I do not want to be a stay-at-home Granny, content in leisured retirement from the world and happy to be exploited as an ever-available carer. I was a stay-at-home mother and arranged my life around the needs of my home and family (as I perceived them) rather than trying to achieve success in the working world and build up a career. This was partly my choice - the direct result, I think, of having spent so much of my childhood in boarding schools, which gave me a strong incentive to create a home and a family of my own as a substitute for my 'deprivation'. These feelings were reinforced by the publication, at the time my children were born, of John Bowlby's work on attachment, stressing the importance of mothers staying at home to look after their young children. And it was possible for educated women to do that thirty-five years ago, without feeling that they were depriving their family of necessities by choosing to be a 'housewife' rather than going out to work.

But looking after small children on one's own all day can be a lonely and demanding occupation, short on intellectual stimulation. I always looked forward to the time when I would have the freedom to pursue my own interests without feeling guilty. I have been slow to get started, but now there are so many things that I want to do. At the same time I am all too conscious that the years of active life left to me are diminishing at what seems like an accelerating rate. I take comfort in the fact that a hundred and fifty years ago, a married woman could expect to live for only two years after her last child left home. For women of my generation (most of whom had their children in their twenties and early thirties), that figure has increased to thirty years. I mean to make good use of my bonus years, to take care of my health and to remain active for as long as possible. So grandparenting time will have to be rationed.

Having said that, what I most care about, and the field to which I would like to make some useful contribution, as a result of my own life experience, is health and quality of life. At the core of health and human happiness is the relationship between parents and their children - and the foundation of that relationship is the bond of attachment that is formed between mother and infant. A baby that feels loved and appreciated, its needs for security and comfort met, will grow up self-confident and feeling good about himself. To have this 'self-esteem', which should be everyone's birthright, is a passport to a happy and healthy life. I'm not saying that those who grow up without it will not overcome this handicap, or that those who have it will inevitably lead a contented and fulfilled life. But all the research shows that individuals whose early upbringing has been unsatisfactory are more likely to suffer from depression, a sense of failure (and thus actual failure) and psychological disorders which may adversely affect their physical health. This is why I became interested in infant massage, which is as much to do with encouraging bonding between mothers (or primary carers) and their babies as it is to do with the physical benefits of the massage itself.

THE IMPORTANCE OF FAMILY

Of course there are a lot of other factors involved in producing healthy and happy human beings. But parenting, I believe, is the most important one, and greatly undervalued and unappreciated in our society. Much research has been done in the past twenty years by behavioural psychologists, ethnographers, social anthropologists, ethologists and even psychotherapists, so that we now have a good idea of the necessary factors for the successful rearing of children who will grow into confident adults, able to enjoy life and perform successfully in the world. I wish I had been more aware of them, and of the effect of my own upbringing on the way I related to my own children, when I was a young parent. There is still a wide gap between the knowledge acquired through research and its application in the field. Although parenting as a skill that can be learned is at last beginning to acquire some credit and parenting classes are proliferating, nevertheless a strong feeling persists that parenting is intuitive and a private matter.

So along with more support for new parents, I would like to see classes in 'emotional intelligence', human relationships and how to manage them, and instruction on the needs of human infants and growing children as a compulsory element in all school curricula.

Modern young women are faced with impossible dilemmas, to a much greater extent, I think, than our generation.

Economic and career pressures are deleterious to family life. Caring for infants and young children is not compatible with total commitment to a demanding full-time job, especially given the long working hours so often required now-a-days. The alternative, a nanny or au-pair, who too often stays only for a few months, or a year at most, cannot provide the kind of attachment figure needed.

I see modern children suffering in just the same way that I did by being sent too early to boarding school. I feel our society has got its priorities wrong. Yes, women should of course have the freedom to work and pursue careers. But if they have children, they should be aware of the kinds of demands which will be made on them and of the importance of fulfilling their offspring's most basic needs for love, attachment and security. And ideally, their partners should take an equal share in child care, in so far as possible. Generous parental leave and support should be provided for by legislation as happens now in some Scandinavian countries.

So I want to do work which raises people's awareness of these problems and can contribute to their alleviation. But if there was a crisis in my own family and I felt that my grandchildren were not getting the care and support that they needed, then I would step in regardless. Ultimately, my family is more important to me than anything else in my life. And this is the legacy I would like to pass on to my grandchildren - a sense of belonging; a pride in their family; a sense of its history and its part in the greater history of the country in which we live. So they feel they have a unique place, a part to play, in the great scheme of things, and they will make their journey through this life on earth with confidence, joy and panache.

LOSING A SON
WITHOUT GAINING A DAUGHTER

Mary Partridge

Becoming a grandmother all happened so suddenly for me that I still can't really believe that Stuart is a father. It only seems like yesterday since he was a baby himself. But I don't think it matters that much that he is so young. He is a good dad and he really loves Jake. He is such a lovely, good baby.

I did worry about it all a bit beforehand. They did not plan it all out. Stuart doesn't really earn that much money, and he has only just started out working with his dad. But she could not have had an abortion, because they felt they could just as easily have the baby. If my daughter Kerry got pregnant I think it would be different. She is doing quite well with her work and I don't think she is as much the family type as Stuart. It has just come a bit earlier than expected for Stuart and Clare. But that is no reason to get rid of it. And that doesn't matter now anyway because they have got this lovely baby and they really love him. They really do.

The birth itself was a bit of a muddle. Clare was round at her mum's when she started to have contractions, and Stuart was not there because he was at work with his Dad, doing the plumbing with him in Birmingham. Clare had been staying quite a bit at her mum's over the last month or so, because it was more comfortable there than the flat for when she was

---

Mary Partridge lives in Warwickshire, where she works as a school dinnerlady. She has two children - Stuart and Kerry - by her second marriage, to Dave, and a grandson - Jake - through Stuart and his girlfriend Clare. Her current partner is Roger.

pregnant. Stuart was not allowed to stay there for some reason, although her parents knew that they were living and sleeping together in the flat.

Clare started having contractions and her mum took her down to the hospital at Southlands and her dad met her there because he works nearby. Anyway they did not tell Stuart or me until they had been there for a couple of hours. Stuart was pretty mad about that actually. He phoned me when he got there, so there was even more of a delay for me and I could not go down there immediately because I was not able to leave work right away.

Dave had to give me a lift. By the time I arrived, Jake had been born already. Clare's parents were the first to hold him after Stuart. So I was pretty pissed off really by the time I got there. Things are a bit difficult between me and Clare's parents at the best of times, so that kind of took over for a while. But when I held the baby in the end, I could not believe it. Before he was born, I had not quite realised what it was going to mean to have another person in the family, and I still didn't think of Stuart as a grown up. But I held the baby and looked at Stuart and thought, "My god, you know, this is really real." And suddenly Stuart seemed like an adult. The funny thing is I found that I just wanted to be around them, and look after them, like a mummy again. And I felt like it was *me* who had had the baby – apart from not feeling all sore and that. I just felt like I wanted to look after them all - Stuart and Jake at any rate. I did not really feel like that towards Clare, because she is not mine I imagine.

I suppose everyone feels like that towards their children's partners, and I have not really got to know Clare that well because she tends to stay away from here and Stuart comes here on his own. I don't really go and see them – especially in the last month or so when Clare was quite far gone and she was round her mum's a bit. And it was not as if there was a marriage really, or anything like that. It was just Stuart and his girlfriend. They did not even live together or anything like that before she fell with Jake. Stuart is still quite young and, although he works now, he has been living at home with me and his brother and sister as a part of this family. It was not like losing a son and gaining a daughter as they say. It was more like losing a son . . . and maybe gaining a grandson.

ON THE OUTSIDE LOOKING IN

It has all been quite hard for me really, and I have not had anyone to talk to about it. Roger doesn't really know Stuart and I don't talk to Dave much because he lives in Birmingham. I suppose that I just thought that when I became a grandma it would all be with us together as a close family. It is not Stuart's fault though. I know it is bit difficult for him too. He was not really prepared for any of this, and he has got to think of Clare and her mum.

The truth is that her mum was not that happy about Clare and Stuart really. I don't know why. She is a bit protective of her daughter and wanted her to go off and go to college I think. The thing is though, Clare was the main one who wanted the baby. She would be quite happy having a family and not having a big career. Sometimes she gets on with me fine I think. But she doesn't really understand us. She is used to a nice big house and things like that, and is a bit scared of seeing people who have to struggle. To be honest I think it is not so much that me and Stuart are not good enough for her, I think that she doesn't want to become like us. She can see from my family that it is pretty hard keeping everything together - that and money and having a bit of a life. She doesn't really understand, although I think she will learn, that just because we live in a smaller house and swear and things like that, we are not really different from them. She thinks we are a bit of a novelty sometimes, but she should not treat people like that. It is not a play. She can't just stand in the wings and judge us. It is real life, and if she was prepared to become part of the family, she would be able to understand that and she might even get something out of it. Her mum fusses around her all the time, and she will always have a bit of money so she doesn't really take on the responsibilities of being in a family – that is, me and Stuart and my lot - because she doesn't need it. I don't want to be horrible about her, but these snooty people, they just think that family means people who give you, or you give them, money. They don't really treat each other like people, so they don't treat *anyone else* like people. I think that having children is all about giving love and showing love. It should make you into a more loving person generally. But if you are a bit selfish to start with, you are going to find it hard to really get that out of your family. Then it transfers to your children, and to other people not in the family. It is a vicious circle.

I don't want Jake to turn out like that. It happens especially to men. They go out and earn money and stay at work all day and they think that is it, that is all you have to do. Because they can buy their way out of responsibility it stops them from taking it and they go off in their own little world. I think all men are like that, not just the ones who live at the top. You don't have to have lots of money to be like that, it just makes it easier if you do I suppose. Acting like that doesn't make you better than everyone else, it means you are not treating people right. Rich or poor, you should not buy your way out of the family. Families ought to be about commitment and involvement in each other's lives.

Families can get messy, and they can be annoying and binding. But you can't just cut off an arm if it doesn't fit in with your ideas of how people should be. It may be a bit funny coming from me with all my divorces. But that is all part of it. I would never cut Dave off from our kids. With all the divorce there is now it is even more important to treat each other like people. The marriage certificate on its own can't bind you. You have to respect people and they will respect you, and hopefully you will carry on like that even if you split up so you can go on helping each other. Being a decent person is more important than anything else, especially marriage. Bad marriages are no excuse for being an arsehole. That is what I think.

THE WAY THINGS USED TO BE

We lived quite close to my own grandmother (my mum's mum) when I was a child. She used to come and visit us every weekend for Sunday tea and that. She was just as much a part of the family as we all were. I don't remember her that well because I was quite young when she died, but I remember her taking us for a walk to the park to feed the ducks. We used to walk all the way up to Priest's Tower before she got too old. I remember her panting and that - though only looking back on it now do I really notice - and we would have to wait for her at the top. And then, it was a bit cruel really, as soon as she got to the top we used to run all the way down. We thought it was a great joke but it was not that good really as she always knew what was coming. But she did it anyway just to give us the satisfaction you know! She was alright I think. In some ways she was always a bit outside the family perhaps, but my mum used to try to keep her inside it, by inviting her around all the time and making sure that she was okay.

My mum now is much more involved in our own family. Although she lives in Birmingham still, we have her over quite a lot – it is only a short drive – and the kids go over to her, or they used to. They don't like it much anymore, but they used to because she had a garden shed with lots of old things in it from my dad. Now, though, they find it a bit of a pain because it usually involves getting up early on a Sunday morning! She has not seen the baby yet which is a real shame as I think she was really looking forward to the next baby in the family. The children don't see Dave's mum or dad very much at all, because they keep themselves to themselves. Now that I live here I suppose that the family has gradually drifted apart. People want to be more independent of their family nowadays. I think it is a bit of a shame, especially with people's mums, because I think it is usually the mum who keeps the rest of the family together.

It may be that because I am the *father*'s mother I am not so involved in the baby's life. Apart from all the stuff with Clare's parents, the fact that they are not really married perhaps means that the link with me is not so strong. When you think about it, the father's parents are not included as much in things generally. But the way that families are changing, with people not really getting married, puts a lot of pressure on grandparents.

Clare's mum even does the washing for her sometimes, and she always tries to take charge of things like injections and that. Her mum *wants* it to be like that! If Clare was a bit older, and they were married, I think that she would get treated like more of an adult. A lot of people I know who are grandparents say the same thing about their children and grandchildren. That is what is changing things most: the not being married. This is more important than the fact that more and more women are working. Work doesn't change it very much. There is no reason why a woman can't work *and* be in charge of the family. And even if it means more pressure on other people, so what? Families need to be involved in each others' lives more. I wish that I had been given the opportunities when I was young that they seem to have now. When *I* was young the only thing that you could do as a girl was be a nurse, or perhaps be a teacher if you were quite good at school. But even then it was expected that you would just get married and have children after a while.

I think it is really good that people have the choice nowadays, although I don't think things have really changed that much. I know a lot of young girls who have had children and who don't want to go to university. There is not much work to do around here anyway. So if you wanted to do something else you would have to move away, and people don't really *want* to move from their families. I was never really that modern myself. I just thought that I would have to get married and have kids, and I never thought of anything else. I really used to look forward to it. It is a shame, because now I have to do a crappy job and there is not much else for us to do around here. But we have to work. I sometimes get a bit upset about it. I don't have a career and marriage has not exactly been what I expected, and I was never caught up in women's lib and burning bras. It was not for me. I felt it was really for those at university. It did not really affect us. I never thought about it that much, neither did any of my friends. It is a shame really, we missed out on the swinging sixties. In the papers there was a lot about 'these stupid women' who were doing this and that. So I suppose that put us off it, and no one told us otherwise.

I wish they had in a way, then I might not be in this situation now.

Countdown to Becoming a Granny for the 21st Century

Ruth Pitt

In July 1999

...I discovered I was to become a grandma literally minutes after my daughter Rebecca did. She called me at our home in Leeds at 10.30 one night – much later than usual – and asked if she and her husband Damien could come round. She sounded excited. Their house is nearby and within minutes they were bursting through my back door armed with a bottle of champagne.

Their faces were radiant in a triumphant sort of way that I can barely describe but will never forget.

"Guess what? We're going to have a baby!"

There were tears and kisses, and my question:

"When did you find out?"

"Ten minutes ago!"

I felt a real sense of humble gratitude that Rebecca had chosen to share this amazing news with me so promptly, because being a mother isn't the easiest thing to get right and I've felt over the years that I've got it wrong often enough. I was only twenty-one when Rebecca was born so we did a lot of our growing up together.

By the time Rebecca was seven I had become a single

Ruth Pitt is editor of the BBC Everyman *series, and runs a TV production company with her partner Ali Rashid. They have two sons and Ruth has a daughter, Rebecca, by her first marriage. They live in Leeds.*

parent who, with no financial support from her father, had to work full-time. There were quite a few years when I think she resented the fact that I wasn't at the school gate like the other mothers, but I felt powerless to change our circumstances. After years of poverty and insecurity, the idea of not working seemed literally life-threatening - and I was determined to carve myself a career as well as a living out of the wreckage of a failed marriage.

We got through it, Rebecca and I. And now here she was: grown up at nearly twenty-six, married, and expecting a baby. And standing in my kitchen with a smile as wide as a mile. The news seemed to signal a closure on me playing the part of 'Mum' and Rebecca playing 'Daughter'. Something new, I sensed immediately, lay ahead.

I went out for a run in the park the following evening and it fully began to dawn on me that the impending arrival could really change not just Rebecca's life but mine too. There was going to be a new person in our family; someone who'd still be very young when I was very old. Someone who would give our family a new stake in the future. It was marvellous, miraculous, and I discovered that as I was running I was laughing my head off.

This was really quite a turn up, because my sense of humour had been seriously taxed over the last few months. My professional workload was becoming unbearable and my hold on everyday activities like supermarket shopping and washing woollens was stretched to its limits. I had been trying to do two jobs – as a documentary strand editor for the BBC and also running a television production company – and it was beginning to dawn on me that something had to give.

The thought of a new baby seemed like a catalyst for change and I determined very early on that I would seize the opportunity to make some changes in my life at the grand old age of forty-six. I decided I could cope with the title 'Grandma', even though it wasn't quite the word I had in mind to describe myself.

IN AUGUST ..

…Not being one to grow old gracefully, I began to explore and possibly redefine what the word 'Grandma' might mean.

I suppose I possess several qualifications for the post of twenty-first century grandparent. I am divorced; I have a professional career; I have a second family. I settled down with my new partner Ali when Rebecca was twelve, and our two beautiful boys Josef and Thomas were born at home. They're now twelve and nearly eleven, and the prospect of having a niece or nephew is a source of constant excitement for them. Rebecca likes the idea too. She watched them both being born so at least she has some idea of what lies ahead!

We went to France on holiday with two other families just after I found out about the new baby, and it was extremely difficult not to tell our friends. But it seemed too soon to be tempting fate. I couldn't stop thinking about it, though, and a real sense of excitement was starting to well up in me.

By the time we got home, Rebecca was already beginning to look different, to change shape slightly. She and Damien were both so thrilled, and we started to discuss the options for a hospital birth and other maternity matters. It all seemed rather odd and yet familiar – like winding the clock back to the days before Rebecca was born nearly twenty-six years ago. Here was the daughter I'd made, and she was about to make someone else!

I went for a run with my friend Rosie and found myself laughing again. "I'm so grateful to Rebecca," I said. "When the boys have left home I'll still have someone young in my life!"

IN SEPTEMBER…

…Rebecca landed on Planet Baby with the commitment of an urban guerilla. I dimly remember feeling the same excitement before she was born, though with the boys I was working in a much more demanding job and didn't stop to reflect as much. But now I found myself rather enjoying her obsession.

We began looking at every kind of catalogue from Argos to Mamas and Papas, and I peeped once again into an entirely female and domestic world that as a working parent I rarely saw these days. Strange questions posed themselves in my head. What kind of grandma would I be? What kind of grandma *could* I be?

I liked Planet Baby a lot more than Planet Wedding, which had been the last major project for Rebecca and me. She and Damien had married on the first of May the previous year, so the baby news had come just three months later.

Planet Wedding had been a trauma. Rebecca wanted the works: white Rolls-Royce, church, sit-down meal, party, big white dress and veil. By contrast, I'd married her father in a rural register office. I'd worn a cream polo-neck jumper and a brown skirt and had driven myself to my own wedding in a seventeen hundredweight Bedford van.

Looking back to my own wedding in January 1973, I can't even quite understand how I made the decision to get married in the first place. I was twenty - it seemed a fun idea. Then soon after the wedding I thought it would be fun to have a baby, and eighteen months later Rebecca was born. How on earth I managed to convince myself I was mature enough to become a parent I shall never quite know. And now here was Rebecca, having a baby of her own. And here was I, about to become a grandma.

My mind galloped back to the day when I'd taken Rebecca into our local bakery when she was just two weeks old. It was June 1974, our first trip out, and I remember that as I queued I had an overwhelming feeling that I could now die happy, having replaced myself with another little person carrying my genes. It was a blissful and liberating sensation, and it was about to repeat itself in my grandchild.

I knew that Rebecca (having watched her two younger brothers grow up) would make the transition to motherhood effortlessly. But would I find the path to grandparenthood as smooth a journey?

I began to think deeply about how I might create a new role for myself in her life.

IN OCTOBER...

...I started to think rather profound thoughts about the purpose of life, the meaning of grandparenthood, the state of the nation and God knows what else. I had sudden panic attacks about my health, realising that I didn't just have to keep myself healthy long enough for my two boys to grow up and leave home, but for a grandchild now too. Remaining fit and active was taking on a much longer term dimension somehow.

I reassured myself I was already pretty fit. I run several miles three times a week and I usually get to the gym on a Sunday to swim with Ali and the boys. I eat well, but after not smoking for seven years when the boys were little, I'd started having the odd fag again. When the pressure of my two jobs started to build up, the smoking had gradually increased to every night.

As Christmas slowly approached and tinsel went on sale in all the shops, images of the new baby grew in my head. I felt sure the new arrival could be the motivation to give up smoking again. New Year's Eve would be the perfect time. Intent on beating the nightly cravings that became daily regrets each morning, I started to prepare myself for the symbolic and badly overdue gesture of quitting for good.

I found myself beginning to focus my own thinking more on to family matters. I wanted to be an active grandma - my own mother had lived 200 miles away while my children were growing up - but then reality began to dawn. How *could* I perform this role? As a thoroughly modern working mother, my days were jam packed with work and every other spare minute was devoted to my sons.

Rebecca had always been fantastically conscientious about popping round to see us, but the new baby was going to mean she'd need a lot more attention and support than a natter on weekdays and breakfast on Sunday mornings. Now I started to get panic attacks about *Finding The Time To Be A Grandma.* Would I really be able to take the pram into the park on a Saturday morning, or would I be too tired to find emotional space for another person in the family?

I remembered my own grandmother. She never had a job from the day she got married, and we lived next door to her. She was always there for us, quietly putting her washing through a hand wringer, grilling chops for grandpa, making cup cakes and drinking sweetened tea. I almost feel she was born with white hair.

Her patience with her grandchildren was infinite. She dressed us up as brides and bridesmaids and pretended to be the vicar so we could imagine ourselves married – every girl's dream in the early 1960's. She wrapped up our dollies and showed us how to hold them properly. She taught us how to make shortbread and to lay the table for tea.

Oh my God! It's only now I'm becoming a grandmother myself that I realise what all the training was about! One thing's for sure; if I have a grand-daughter I certainly won't be teaching her how to iron shirts.

I would have to be such a different kind of grandma. I can't do that domestic stuff, though I adored my grandmother for her selfless devotion to her family. No, I would have to redefine the meaning of the word, so that I could be a good grandma but one that matched the reality of the modern world.

IN NOVEMBER...

...Rebecca and I went shopping for a pram. I was staggered at the choice. And the cost. But she'd already been extensively researching pram and pushchair technology for quite a few weeks, so she knew exactly what she wanted. The sales assistant assembled the combination of frame, carry cot and pushchair she'd chosen. Rebecca had a go at pushing it round the showroom and we both laughed. Then I had a go too. My spirit leapt! I wanted to push the pram right out of the shop and push it all the way home and then keep pushing it until the baby was born.

Yes, we really were going to have a baby. We put a down payment on the pram and agreed to pick it up after Christmas.

IN DECEMBER...

...I finally got used to all my friends and work colleagues saying, "You're too young to be a grandma," or, "You can't be serious!" This is not because I am, strictly speaking, too young to be a grandma at all. I shall be forty-seven when Rebecca's baby is born, which hardly qualifies me for the title of Britain's Youngest Grandma. But I suppose I don't look like the grandmas that my friends had themselves.

And I definitely don't think I behave like a grandma in waiting. The fact that I can run (almost) as fast as my twelve year old son may give you an inkling of my largely ungracious determination to fight the years. I harbour (and often indulge) a secret passion for Prada, love a night out on the town with the girls and have regularly been known to dance till dawn.

Does this mean I'm too young to be a grandma? Clearly the age isn't the issue. It's not that I don't look like a grandmother at all. *This is* what twenty first-century grandmothers *will* look like, and this is what they'll *be* like too.

I started to feel a whole lot better about being called 'Grandma' once I'd worked out what the word could mean in the year 2000.

IN JANUARY 2000...

...We collected the new pram and brought it home. I began to get seriously excited, and the fine detail of Rebecca's ante-natal reports became more and more central to my life. The two of us did, however, make one or two concessions to her husband. We bought the plainest pram in the known universe, and Rebecca opted for a loosely matching Nike shoulder bag for the nappies - to save him the embarrassment of embroidered rabbits as he prepared for fatherhood.

But the biggest concession of all was quitting smoking. I managed it for years when my own babies were born, and the prospect of a grandchild gave me the impetus I needed to kick the habit again. I had my last cigarette on New Year's Eve.

In February...

...Two extraordinary things happened. First, I discovered that grandmothers begin to nest like mothers do. I clambered to the top of the linen cupboard and discovered baby bed linen I hadn't seen for over a decade. I pulled out blankets that had been used in my own cot over forty-five years ago, and I even washed a baby sling that had been used to carry Rebecca as a baby. I delved into the cellar and dragged out the swinging crib (in which not just my own boys but no less that eight friends' babies had slept in the interim).

The second change in me was noted with no small degree of glee by my friends. I went up a cup size in sympathy with my daughter's rapidly expanding bosom. Now you may be sceptical about this, but I hereby commend myself to scientific research for the purpose of testing such a claim. I have to say, as one who has for a lifetime (excluding pregnancy and breastfeeding) been consigned to the unhappy fate of a 32B cup bra, this was a most wonderful development.

In March...

...I realised I had to make urgent plans to stay close by. I wanted to be there if Rebecca needed me at the birth. My own grandmother rarely ventured further than the local shops just a mile away, but my work frequently took me to London, Scotland, Manchester and even overseas. I would have to ensure that all my meetings could be cancelled at short notice for at least the coming six weeks.

Rebecca started calling daily. She was calm, healthy, optimistic. I was full of admiration and pride. My baby was making a baby – and she was doing really well! She was now on maternity leave from her job at a local advertising agency, but she didn't miss work for a minute and seemed not the slightest bit interested in returning. Her determination to be a full-time mother made me feel that maybe she had spectated my efforts to hold down a job and bring her up – and had vowed never to do the same.

Did this mean that I'd failed as a mother? I agonised over the possibility. Was I about to become one of those women who had chosen full-time work alongside motherhood, only to regret it bitterly when it was too late to turn the clock back?

I looked at my two beautiful sons. Healthy, happy, balanced, kind. I looked at Rebecca. Confident, fit as a butcher's dog, single-minded – and wanting me to be there for her. My own children, I realised, were confirmation that I hadn't done too badly.

I began to believe that I *could* be the Grandma I wanted to be after all.

IN APRIL...

...The most beautiful baby in the world, my grandson Sam, was born. He arrived just two hours after his due-date and the birth was perfect. Rebecca called me at 9.30pm to say that she was in labour but felt fine, and was about to leave home for the hospital. She promised that Damien would call on the mobile the second things got difficult. I was five minutes away. I cried, but they were happy tears of expectation. I told my partner Ali and my boys and we all began to prepare ourselves for the big news.

I moped around the house for the rest of the evening and then went to bed. I convinced myself that they'd probably discovered it was a false labour and had come home again. Or that the baby wouldn't be born for another twenty-four hours. I went to bed and drifted off to sleep.

Suddenly something as certain as an explosion woke me up. I sat bolt upright in bed and heard Rebecca calling out. I absolutely did. The alarm clock said 1.44 am. I sat there, mentally in the room with her, feeling so stunningly close to her that my heart was thudding.

Half an hour later I was still wide awake when the phone rang. Leaping from my bed, I grabbed the receiver and blundered "What? What?"

Rebecca's voice was calm and clear. "It's me, Mum. I've had a baby boy. He's fantastic and it was brilliant. I want to do it again!"

She was still in the delivery room. It had all been over in five hours. No panic, no stitches. A tiny and beautiful boy, weighing 6lb 2oz. The time of birth was recorded at 1.46 am, just two minutes after I'd woken. The deep, almost primitive power of motherhood had asserted itself on us both.

I told my delighted family and then sat on the stairs and cried my eyes out.

AN EPILOGUE

And now Sam is nearly two weeks old. I first set eyes on him just hours after he was born and it was love at first sight. He's thriving on the breastmilk Rebecca so graciously provides for him and she's coping quite brilliantly. I know she's been helped by watching her two brothers born and raised, and I know that she has learned how to love and care for her own baby because of the love she's known herself.

My life feels irrevocably changed. There is a new person in our family and we have all shifted our roles to a new and slightly better place as a result.

I have reorganised my work schedule to allow myself two days per week of working from home. I have borrowed a pushchair, a high chair and a cot so that Rebecca doesn't need to bring lots of baby paraphernalia when she visits. I have taken my grandson proudly into the park in his pram, and I have already discovered that when I sing to him he thinks it's the most wonderful sound in the world.

I'm still not smoking. People who know me say I look healthier, happier, younger. And I believe I know why. I have discovered, yet again, that children give one more reasons to be cheerful than any other aspect of this transient life of ours can ever do. And that's as true in the twenty-first century as it's been throughout time.

GRANDMOTHERS-IN-WAITING

CONTEMPLATING GRANDMOTHERHOOD

Janet L Nelson

Betwixt-and-between times are always unsettling. For me, between knowing I was to become a grandmother and actually becoming one, is proving such a time. It has caught me by surprise: not because the news of the forthcoming baby was surprising, for Lizzie and Hugh, ever since they married nearly four years ago, had always envisaged having children, nor because the implications for me were wholly unexpected, for we had discussed well beforehand my sharing of the childcare, but because the prospect of grandmotherhood has turned out to mean much more in my life than I had imagined. The meanings are multiple, and therefore far from straightforward. Disentangling them has not been easy.

Perhaps at this point, I ought to say that I deeply share many of them with my husband, but because he spends much time abroad, my contemplation of grandparenthood has been largely solitary. I think it's also been gender-specific, for reasons I'll try to explain. My thinking has been inescapably influenced, too, by my own work as a medieval historian, and latterly a historian of women and the family, and also by my life as a teacher of students who have included, among the mature ones, many mothers and grandmothers. For me, our

Janet L Nelson is Professor of Medieval History at King's College London. *She recently became Vice-President (Humanities) of the* British Academy, *and President-elect of the* Royal Historical Society. *Her first grandchild was due in July 2000. She lives in East Dulwich, south London.*

shared experiences have always been an important source of support. The same goes for my colleagues, including some of the men as well as some of the women among them. Here, anyway, are three meanings of prospective grandmotherhood, as I have perceived them, distinctly, yet simultaneously.

1   DELIGHT IN A RECURRING THOUGHT

I recall as a young woman finding child-birth and small children in general faintly boring, sometimes repellent, as topics of conversation and even in the flesh. How little I knew! Having babies of my own opened my mind to a whole new realm of experience and sympathy. Love of my own little ones turned out quite naturally to be expandable to nieces and nephews, the children of friends, and babies in general. I had read, before becoming a mother, St Augustine's reaction to tiny infants in the Confessions, but this had never struck me as surprising, or sad. After having babies, I was shocked to re-read what Augustine wrote: 'I have seen a baby jealous ... livid with rage as it saw another baby at the breast': the baby as the very reverse of a little innocent, but, instead, the embodiment of greed, envy, anger, in short, of original sin. I imagined the venerable bishop peering into a cradle, terrifying some tiny infant, and 'reading' his or her wilfulness in the light of orthodox doctrine. Perhaps Augustine would have seen no differently if that baby had smiled... but I like to imagine that he might have.

Whether or not smiles are expected and met with (and a complete stranger probably ought not to expect them), babies seem to signify that the world can be a smiling place. Babies' defencelessness brings out the gentle and protective in most people, and, if you are a parent yourself, reminders of the time, however long since, when your parenthood was new. For me, the prospect of my daughter's motherhood has evoked deep memories of her, and her brother's, babyhoods, and so, of my own pregnancies and child-bearings. These memories are almost entirely happy ones, and happiness pervades my contemplation of the new birth itself. Not a day has passed since last December without the thought of the expected grandchild coming into my head, and making me smile. Since January, three scan-pictures have been sellotaped to the side of my office computer. Every day, I confront a great mystery.

Historically, this liminal, expectant, phase, which was something nearly all women experienced, was a time of cruel anxiety as well as of happiness. For until barely more than a century ago in western Europe, and still in much of the third world, giving birth was both an experience of unrelieved pain, and a time of serious danger for mother and child. Not only was infant mortality horrendously high. Of women who died during their childbearing years, perhaps one in four died in childbed.

Social class made little or no difference to the risk, and the risk remained as high with successive deliveries. A prospective mother's mixed feelings included a strong element of fear. So too must a prospective grandmother's have done. Yet prospective grandmothers, given low levels of life expectancy, may not have been so thick on the ground in the European past. Out of 3,404 recorded women in an early ninth-century survey of peasant families near Paris, just 26 (1.3%) were grandmothers.

Grandmothers of any kind are extraordinarily poorly documented in the modern historiography of women, and it may be that grandmotherhood, historically, is not a very large subject - which does not mean that it was an insignificant one: the late medieval popularity of devotional images of a three-generational family, St Anne, holding a book, her daughter the youthful Virgin Mary, and the infant Jesus, says something about perceptions of grandmotherhood in northern Europe on the eve of the Reformation. Such prospective grandmothers as there ever were must, anyway, have shared the fears and anxieties of their pregnant daughters and daughters-in-law. Times have changed: the waiting time can be a time of almost unqualified joy - though even now, I have to admit, honestly, to twinges of old-fashioned anxiety. Joy, though, was certainly my first, and has remained my chief, response to imminent grandmotherhood: joy, and the confronting of mystery.

2 TIES THAT BIND

In these recent months, I have thought much about the family, in fact about multiple families, my daughter Lizzie's, and her husband Hugh's, my own and my husband's. Our families have always been very important to me and my husband. We named our children with family-names. Just as I and my sisters were given our mother's maiden-name as our middle-name, so my maiden-name was given to my daughter. Family traits and resemblances have always intrigued me. Always strongly aware of a sense of a family-line stretching back into the past, I now foresee it extending by another generation into the future. I share delight in this prospect not only with my husband, but with the other grandparents-to-be, Hugh's parents, with whom over the past few years a friendship has grown, and also with my parents-in-law, now in their mid-eighties and, happily, enchanted by the thought of great-grandparenthood.

My feelings are complicated by rekindled regret about the absence of my own parents, my father who died long ago aged only fifty-five, my mother who died ten years ago, at eighty. Their lives, and their deaths, have come quite often into my mind in recent months. Then there is a sharper regret that my mother's long ill-health never allowed her to be a very active grandmother. Beyond that are memories of my own grandmother, the only grandparent I ever knew, an Ayrshirewoman with a wicked sense of humour whose favourite songs, sung with gusto to regale her grandchildren, were, 'Roll out the barrel! We'll have a barrel of fun!' and 'Ye cannie shove yer granny off the bus!'

Lizzie's way of thinking about the family is not the same as mine or my husband's, nor is Hugh's like that of his parents.

The perpetuation of family surnames, for instance, means little to either of the young ones. Yet in her own way Lizzie has a very deep sense of family, especially of its women. She talks to me of how she would bring up a daughter, if a daughter it is (they have chosen not to know, in traditional fashion, the sex of their unborn child, though the scan made the information available to the doctors); and telling stories about the aunts and great-aunts is set to be an important theme, of which, to my surprise, she's more keenly aware than I am myself. Whether this baby is a girl or a boy, what matters to Lizzie and Hugh is to pass on the interest and variety of lived lives, not traditions or signs of distinction. The family is to be strengthened not only, nor even primarily, in a linear way, but laterally and diversely. In these conversations and anticipations, I find new ties that bind, and will bind, me to my daughter and son-in-law, and, all being well, to the child to come.

3   THE PROSPECT OF CARING

Thinking about my own maternity, I relive more than regret - a kind of anguish - at having left my children in the care of child-minders. However conscientious those minders were, they could not, I knew at the time, provide the love, nor the companionship, that I or my husband could have done. We both worked, were both at the early stages of careers. In the early '70s, it would never have been expected that a man would give up work to care for children, nor, frankly, did it ever cross our minds. My husband went early to work in order nearly always to be home by 5.30. He made the very most of the evening hours of fathering. And I? As an academic, I had fairly flexible hours, especially in vacations. Yet it has been the one big regret in my life that I could not have been with my children full-time when they were very young.

Would I have chosen differently had I time over again? I doubt it. I was convinced that if I gave up my job, I would

never get back into my career. And I was ambitious. None of
the women who'd taught me, inspirationally, at my women's
college had children. My generation wanted it both ways. We
would have career and children. But except in the early months
of my children's lives, which I remember as uniquely joyful,
there was always a tension between goods. I wished, certainly
unreasonably, that my mother could have helped me; but the
reality of the situation was that she needed *my* help. Lizzie in
her early months became a star-turn as a twice-weekly visitor
to the Bethlem Hospital, bringing cheer to unhappy patients
including my mother.

I think it was then, in Lizzie's early years, that I made a
private resolve that when the time came, I would do what I
could, if we lived close enough, to make up to her for what I
still can't help feeling as my own partial failure, and help her
to square the circle. Better still, I would break out of what I
have since suspected was a generations-old cycle of maternal
frustration. My own mother had never let us forget that she
had given up a potential career to be a wife and mother. That
was the burden she laid on her daughters, and I think her own
mother had done likewise. My children have been spared that,
yet guilt and unresolved tension may be the no less
burdensome impositions of my generation on our offspring.

When Lizzie was some three weeks old, my husband and I
happened to be listening to the radio as I was breastfeeding
her. What we heard was an Advent sermon of Augustine on
the theme of Christ's Nativity. The one certain implication of
this child's being born a human child, like every one of us,
said Augustine, was, and is, mortality. The one certain thing
about the infant - any infant - is that, having been born, he or
she will one day die. These words, that struck me with
unforgettable, painful force as I looked on my baby, are as true
now as sixteen hundred years ago. I drew no Augustinian
inference about original sin. I inferred, instead, an
overwhelming human need to make each life, and perhaps most
of all the lives of my own children, as good in their living as

possible, and as unburdened. Putting that perception into practice is, as everyone knows, the tricky bit.

In the intervening twenty-odd years since I was a young mother, much has changed, and, in terms of social context, surely for the better. Part-time work even in professional careers has become feasible; relationships between husbands and wives have become more genuinely equal. Both Lizzie and Hugh contemplate working three days a week; they're lucky enough to have secure jobs, and they have bought a house within ten minutes' drive of mine. In my own life, since the children were teenagers, work has become even more demanding. Seven days a week has been normality for some time (as it certainly is, ambition apart, for a fair number of senior academics). Yet I have committed myself to a new normality in the future, devoting one day each week to caring for my grandchild.

When I told Lizzie and Hugh of this decision, they were amazed, but delighted. Most of my colleagues and friends have been amazed, and faintly incredulous, since my professional life, perhaps inevitably, continues to produce new responsibilities. I prepare to become a grandmother with a certain trepidation, not just because I'm in need of retraining in so many practical tasks, not just because I fear, as the grandchild (and grandchildren?) grow(s) a little older, I may get tired more quickly, and find it hard to keep up with their energy, not just because I worry about displeasing Lizzie and Hugh inadvertently (for my idea of course is to follow their line) over such small matters as the grandchild's feeding, entertainments, discipline: but because my intent is to change my life, by precisely one day a week - and that, in occasional moments' loss of nerve, seems a wild venture.

Mostly, though, I view this venture, this other change of life, with optimism that I hope tempers grannyish rolling-out of the barrel with sobriety. I am in the processing of shedding, as well as acquiring, work-tasks, and my forward planning keeps Thursdays free. The sense of joy, and the consciousness of family solidarities, have grown as the months passed. The understanding and shared commitment between Lizzie and Hugh on the one hand, me on the other, are close; and my husband's support will be there for all of us, not least during the birth itself, for the plan is that the baby will be born at home, with grandparental as well as paternal assistance for mother and midwife.

The next generation, Lizzie's and Hugh's, may not have it easier than ours, but they will surely have more choices, amid more freedom from fixed gender roles, new configurations of families, and planned residential proximity of parents and adult children. Maybe this one grandmother's new role will prove symptomatic of a new age of grandparents in the early twenty-first century?

When I was twenty, and a dear older friend told me cheerfully, "Life begins at fifty," I laughed. I've since found that life has begun anew quite a few times. It promises to do so again in July, 2000, as, all being well, the new grandchild's life in the big wide world begins.

THE GRANDMOTHER *MANQUÉ*

Julienne Ford

WAITING FOR THE CALL

What might grandmotherly feelings be like that I might know them? After all even motherliness was never my strong point though, perversely, I was indeed the earth-mother for a surprisingly resilient community of adults and kids. Yet I never really saw myself as a mother, even though parenthood was my dominant identity and the rationale for all my other roles and statuses. I've always been so over-ridingly *ideological* that when I fiercely maintained that I had no interest in biological, but only in cultural, reproduction, I did actually mean it. And I still do.

You hear people speaking of becoming grandmothers as a magical form of gratification, all the pleasure (pride) and none of the pain (shame) of actual parenthood. I know that these are feelings I will never have, because they stem from a desire to reproduce oneself physically and an aggrandisement of family which I had already rejected in my teens. Engel's *Holy Family* liberated (or estranged?) me from this framework of emotions in a very permanent way. To me, the sacrifices we make for

Julienne Ford is a sociologist and writer who divides her time between rural Wales and East London. Her books include Paradigms and Fairy Tales, Human Wave *and* Social Class and the Comprehensive School. *She has a son, Jim, who lives mainly in Manchester with his girlfriend, and two step-grandchildren through her first marriage. But she is still 'in-waiting' for a blood grandchild.*

our children and grandchildren are not forms of altruism but simply baroque versions of selfishness. To embrace the role of grandparent, let along grand*mother*, I would need to be able to feel grandmotherly towards an entire generation.

But I am not ready for that yet. I don't feel anywhere near old enough. Most of my middle-class friends have children in their late twenties like me, but none of them are grandparents. The only grandparents among them are at least a decade older. Yet biologically I am old enough to be a great-great-grandmother. (One could be a mother at fourteen, grandmother at twenty-eight, great-grandmother at forty-two and, yes by fifty-six - which I nearly am - a great-great-grandmother.) This is another way of asserting the continuing irrelevance of biological reductionism in my life.

A HIPPY MATRIARCH

In fact my actual grandchildren, Tom and Lucy, have not a single genetic link to me *or* my own biological offspring. My first husband had a daughter at seventeen with a woman who subsequently 'ran away with a sailor'. The girl was raised as his sister but is (or rather was, as I had already divorced him before he died) technically my step-daughter, though she never felt like it and still does not. Unfortunately she had a hysterectomy in her early thirties at which time she did not think she wanted children anyway. Later she changed her mind and adopted the angelic pair who in a remote and unreal way confer on me the status of grandmother.

So here you have the limiting case, the grandmother *manqué*, who cannot scrape together the slightest shred of pride in the status, biological or otherwise. And this is how I want it to be because by definition grandmothers must be reactionary and I still manage to kid myself that I am a permanent ideological revolutionary.

My view is that, when considering industrial societies, except in a small number of cases of genuine tragedy, the close involvement of grandmothers in the daily responsibility for and care of their grandchildren represents outstanding failure the first time around. I was raised by a grandmother because my mother, never having read Sartre, did not realise the extent to which she was responsible for her own decisions. She had not the sense to anticipate the consequences of marriage to an RAF warrant officer who would be posted all over the place. This meant that, apart from a brief period in married quarters in Germany, she would effectively be a single parent, a role for which she had neither the intellectual nor the spiritual resources. She in fact failed in her motherhood just as surely, and in her own prim manner just as fecklessly, as the three teenage babymothers of my Rastafarian boyfriend's seven children. All of these, like the overwhelming majority of the children on this sink estate in East London, are being raised by their maternal grandmothers. In other words these children are being socialised by women who have already failed at motherhood.

Warming to my self-justificatory theme I am now going on to assert that, despite the bizarre family-negating sixties culture that I co-invented during my own child-raising period, I did not fail in parenting. This I claim is shown by the fact that my biological offspring does not take reproduction lightly and holds back from producing babies precisely because he is daunted by the level of responsibility and self-sacrifice which he feels parenting requires. The rest of the five children I raised are not biologically related to me but neither they nor the five half-siblings of my biological son have produced any children yet.

The little hippy tribe of which I am still proud matriach has been singularly unproductive as a unit of population. Good for us I say. I am well proud of that. There are far too many humans on the planet, particularly in the Northern hemisphere where each child born is likely to use the equivalent in terms of the earth's resources of ten children from the Southern hemisphere.

CULTURE VERSUS BIOLOGY

Cultural reproduction on the other hand should know no such restraints. After all, if you are happy enough with your own micro-culture and ideology to carry on keeping faith with it then surely you should be able to make a Kantian categorial imperative into an actuality!

Being a teacher in higher education I had better opportunity than most to propagate my ideas. Indeed it is still immensely gratifying that ex-students (most of them now themselves *in loco parentis* for the grandchild generation) still contact me to renew their gratitude for the way their worldviews and lifechances changed.

Indeed for a little while in the 1970s it did seem that we were at last winning the war against all the tyrannies of status ascription: racism, sexism, ageism, tribalism, familism - all those monstrous institutions of genetic mumbo-jumbo - were at last beginning to be perceived as crumbling ruins along the road to reason/freedom. Then while we grandmothers of the revolution were chilling out and congratulating ourselves, Margaret ('we are a grandmother') Thatcher, the ultimate ideological milk-snatcher, came up from behind and hand-bagged everything good and decent and hopeful to pulp. The wicked step-gran made short work of socialism, solidarity, altruism, internationalism, respect for the planet, respect for each other, and most particularly respect for the rights of children to self-determination.

She even demolished the deferred gratification which had always been at the core of the Protestant Ethic that had previously been regarded as the *sine qua non* of capitalism itself. The New Right trumpeted the heroism of hedonism and peddled the ego-porn culture in which 'Access' took 'the waiting out of wanting', stock market booms and busts and privatisation bonanzas were oiled by cocaine; the L'Oréal can make every granny look like magazine masturbation fodder, "Because I'm worth it."

THE STOLEN GENERATION

The result has been an epidemic of 'attention deficit hyperactivity disorder' among the grandchildren who are required to sit in front of a cathode ray tube consuming pernicious propaganda or virtually participating in sport, pseudo-education or aggressive video games via technology that exercises only their thumbs. If they leave the TV screen to go outside the house (say to a theme park, intelligence-suppressing school or the Millennium Dome) they must be driven everywhere by car. Thus the fear of imaginary stranger-monsters traps them in the *familiar* environment of genetic and cultural reproduction where the real abuse takes place. So, subdued by Ritalin, junk food, TV and the hideous straight-jackets of activity-restraining designer 'sports' gear, this generation is being prepared for the function of consumption just as surely as their grandparents were brainwashed for their roles in the production process.

Only the aristocracy and the underclass are spared this particular form of parental and grandparental abuse. In the absence of interference by their families, these groups are free to get on with the real business of abusing, or being abused by, their peers and the scapegoat victims of their very different styles of blood sports.

As I marinade my feet in the urine, broken glass and blood going down towards the ground in the lift, I know how lucky I was that my children were free to climb out of the windows and run in the woods. I only hope they will have some of that free spirit left to share with a generation that is missing out on childhood, whether they produce further grandchildren for me or not. Meanwhile I must keep reminding myself that grandmothers have a serious and important role to play: looking on the bright side of life!

WAITING FAIRLY PATIENTLY

Kirsteen Tait

I am not yet a grandmother, though as I do have grown-up children I could become one at any time now. As I wait, I have time to brood over several issues. These were not always there. Changes in family life mean that quite a few things are not nearly as straightforward today as they must have been once.

COUNTING THE STEPS

The first issues are matters of definition. What actually counts as a grandparental relationship these days? Different lifestyles, not to mention the new demographics, have made it all much more complicated.

I can only remember one out of four grandparents, though two were alive when I was born. My children only knew one and one step. Yet if my daughter had a baby this year, it could have as many as eight - if the baby's father had divorced parents too. The mathematics have been changed dramatically by divorce and longer lives. But the question is: do steps count as one, or a half?

Kirsteen Tait is involved in a number of voluntary sector activities. She is Chairman of the British Dyslexia Association, *and is currently working to set up an independent agency dealing with refugee issues. She has three children from her first marriage and lives in London with her second husband who has five.*

From a statistical point of view I am likely to enter grandparenthood through marriage; having five step-children, mostly older than my own. It'll be very interesting to see how it turns out. We have eight children between us (me three from one marriage, he five from two). They range in age from seventeen to thirty-seven. Four boys, four girls. None married, none with children. Seven out of the eight are in steady relationships. If each of them eventually had the notional average of 2.4 I could have about nineteen grandchildren. But will I count for a whole grandmother in the eyes of the steps?

The truth is that the questions dominate while you are waiting. It is the vacuum, the going on holiday with contemporaries who spend hours choosing baby clothes with expensive smocking in dark Spanish stores. This feeds the questions and doubts. If I was already a grandmother I'd know the answers instinctively and be too busy to think about them. One day one of them will have a baby and these questions will evaporate.

But why *haven't* I got any grandchildren yet?

CHOICE, AND UNCERTAINTY

This leads into more questions, which are bound up with our greater choice over the roles we play. In an age of growing flexibility in family life, what determines the desire to become a parent, and also a parent's feelings about being a grandparent? Might it be my fault in some way that I am not a grandmother? My younger sister has a grandchild. My husband's younger sister has five - plus twins expected this summer. It's clearly not a matter of age of children. Is it just chance?

How far may our missing grandchildren be explained by our own broken marriages? Are our children failing to marry because they have seen so clearly the pitfalls? Will they wait so long to be sure that the urge passes them by? But looking around my friends and relations, some of the children of divorce have married young - some out of deprivation, some defiantly, many quite ordinarily.

Divorce does spill over into everything. It doesn't spare grandmothering. All the guilt and insecurity returns - but in a new form. Will my children's children want me? Have time for me on their birthdays? Will our children prefer to leave their babies in the care of others within the complex family line-ups? Will the poor babies get divided up too thinly?

When we complain to our friends or joke about paying one of our offspring to have a child, we are invariably told that it will be the other way round. They will all give birth in the same year and we'll have to run a creche to cope with the demands for baby sitting. The working lives of the daughters and the sons' girlfriends will thrust a role on us.

The mystery to me in this is why I - now fifty-eight - can begin to feel that I might like to run a creche for them. It's the last thing I would have done when my children were small. Making room for regular babysitting and childminding would mean changing my working life drastically. So why is the role so alluring? Is it the luxury of being allowed to do some of what you missed out on with your own children through anxiety and exhaustion. Or to try something new? There was a period when all they wanted to do were the things that I lacked talent and patience for - singing, playdough etc. Yet I'm quite keen to tackle that now. Do I perhaps want a second chance to play a role in that stage between babyhood and, say, about two-and-a-half when you can first have a conversation with them?

My own children rejected attractive clothes at a very early age, and it was both extravagent and pointless to buy them. As a grandmother you can disregard all that and just do it. In much more important ways, too, you might be able to make up for the extravagances you missed out on as parents - more time to play, to investigate things in the street, to laugh. I register the difference between the mothers and fathers taking their children to childminders and nurseries - unresponsive, striding out, mind half on the In-Tray - and the dawdling grandparents, hand in hand with the toddler absorbed in contemplation of the empty crisp packet on the pavement. Compensating for self-inflicted emotional deprivation as a parent? Or are these the grandparents who were patient and relaxed as parents?

But the deprivation model cannot explain the appetite and the fascination. It is partly a facet of wanting to be useful to your children, easing their busy stressful lives - alongside lending them your car, advising on annuals for their patios, discussing their work problems. "I'll take the baby and you have a nice rest, go out and buy yourself a new T-shirt etc." That impulse to shoulder sons' and daughters' cares, fully exercised without babies, will take a new turn.

It's not just that. It's what you've learnt in the meantime about the world and the confidence you've gathered with the years. You can see that the things that you made a great fuss about don't matter at all - "Take a sweater"; "You've got to eat that apple before the Jaffa cake"; "If you're not well enough to go to school you're not well enough to watch telly". And the things that did matter that you got wrong - not allowing the child to sleep in your bed at the right moments, supporting the mean-spirited and misguided teacher, underestimating A-levels and exaggerating sex and drugs.

KNOWING WHAT IS RIGHT

Then questions start to arise about how far we can, or should, follow these impulses. Grandparents are said to spoil their grandchildren, though I doubt if it is quite that. They know that very little that happens is irretrievable except neglect. They have seen their own and friends' children get into trouble and cope with setbacks, progress too slowly in some ways and too fast in others, and that it more or less sorts itself out in most cases. That perspective is their contribution.

But there are the discipline grandmothers. They say they provide routine and structure because the parents don't. Will I be a perspective grandmother or a discipline grandmother? There's no contest. But then I was an anxious parent and I've got a lot of ground to make up.

And central to being a grandmother are the claims of the past and the future. You are the pivot between your own grandparents and great-grandparents in the photograph album, and the new generations. You make a small contribution to a world generally starved of history. Not passing on cumulative memories must be the hardest part of accepting that your children are not going to have children.

Two of my friends and exact contemporaries at university have died of cancer within the last year. One had two grandchildren whom she adored, and for whom she was immensely important. She desperately wanted to know what happened next. The other left one daughter recently married with the other recently engaged. At her funeral her husband, himself a vicar, said that we should console ourselves that of the two roles - mothering and grandmothering - the first was immensely the more important, and that she had been outstanding. Of course being a parent is *more* important; but that is exactly why being a grandparent *is* so important. His consolation is really no consolation.

I'm not exactly practicing, but five of my eight god-daughters and one of my three godsons have children and I hold their new babies with pleasure and pride. Now my own children are becoming godparents and they email me films of them. Is it just that babies are so nice, or do they have to be in your line? You could be in trouble for soliciting strange babies in the street.

STAYING PATIENT

I'm not desperate either. I'm just really looking forward to it. Some women I know are renewed by grandchildren and become almost totally preoccupied. Others are guarded and somehow disconcerted. My own mother was like that - at first.

She came to stay with me in Belgrade when I emerged from the National Gynaecological Hospital with my daughter, born breech without anaesthetics and swaddled into immobility in Serbian style. She seemed to be doing her duty to her first grandchild. But later they adored each other. She was a good woman and a strong influence.

Her mother was not so obviously a good woman. A beauty, spoilt perhaps, self-willed and arbitrary, unable to boil an egg, impatient with children, she nonetheless created whatever the extraordinary bond is. She belonged to me and was uncritically loyal, while not otherwise being famous for those qualities. She brought me history, and another point of view. It was her sharing with me her audacious past that cemented the link.

Perhaps in the end that's what you get. The chance to recreate yourself for your childrens' babies in the image you want. And it could just be better than the reality you've been stuck with so far.

APPENDICES

NOTES

1   [page x] See Dench, Ogg & Thomson, 1999.

2   [x] I have argued this at greater length in 'Nearing full circle in the sexual revolution', in Dench, 1997.

3   [xi] See Hrdy, 1999.

4   [xii] Bloch, 1953 pp 40/1.

5   [xiii] Dench, 1996.

6   [xv] The exception is Nell Dunn, who in reality has been a granny for more than ten years. However, when the material in her chapter was originally written her first grandchild was still only two. This is what is relevant to the experiences and sentiments underlying the writing. So this is where she has been placed in the collection.

7   [xvi] This was still true in the 'old' Bethnal Green explored by Michael Young and Peter Willmott (1957). Grandmothers, known as 'Mum', were at the centre of community life, where they exercised considerable influence not just over family affairs and personal relations but also practical matters of employment and housing. They occupied a pedestal of respect which no politician (and few men) could hope to emulate.

8   [xvi] As shown for example in the work in France of Claudine Attias-Donfut (1998) who is herself a contributor to this volume.

9   [xvi] See Mount, 1982.

10   [xvii] Dench, 1997, p 54.

11   [1] For further information on this see Erin Pizzey, 'Why did my grandson die?', *The Observer*, 9th April 2000.

12   [7] In *Anna Karenina*, pt 1 ch 1.

13   [40] See Bryan *et al.*, 1982.

14   [41] i.e Bernie Grant, MP.

15   [79] In *The Observer*, 7th November, 1999.

16   [79] quoted in the same article.

17   [91] I welcome the work now being done by the *Family Policy Studies Centre* and the *Institute of Community Studies* which will throw more light on all of this.

18   [91] See McGlone et al., 1998.

19   [108] See Dench, Ogg & Thomson, 1999.

20   [108] The Grandparents' Federation can be contacted on 01279   444964.

21   [110] See Neugarten & Weinstein, 1964.

22   [110] McGlone *et al.*, 1999, p 8.

23   [138] Translated into English by Jim Ogg.

24   [148] This chapter is composed of extracts taken from Nell Dunn's book *Talking to Grandmothers*, published by Chatto and Windus in 1991.

REFERENCES

Attias-Donfut C & M Segalen (1998) *Grands-Parents: la famille à travers les générations*, Paris: Odile Jacob.

Bloch M (1953) *The historian's craft*, New York: Vintage.

Bryan B *et al.* (1982) *The heart of the race*, London: Virago.

Dench G (1996) *Transforming men*, New Brunswick: Transaction.

"   (Ed) (1997) *Rewriting the sexual contract*, New Brunswick: Transaction.

"   & J Ogg & K Thomson (1999) 'The role of grandparents', in R Jowell *et al.*, *British Social Attitudes, the 16th Report, Who Shares New Labour Values?* Aldershot: Ashgate.

Hrdy S B (1999) *Mother nature*, London: Chatto & Windus.

McGlone F, A Park & K Smith (1996) *Families & kinship*, London: FPSC.

"   (1999) 'A new role for grandparents', *Family Policy*, Bulletin of the Family Policy Studies Centre, London.

Mount F (1982) *The subversive family*, London: Cape.

Neugarten B & K Weinstein (1964) 'The changing American grandparent', *Journal of Marriage and the Family*, 26:2.

Young M & P Willmott (1957) *Family and kinship in East London*, London: Routledge & Kegan Paul.